A Beginner's Guide to Second Life
By v3image

BOOK 1: Version 1.1 (5/2007)

In-World Acknowledgements

Special thanks to the Second Life Residents Tara Anna, Ralph Kearby, Phillip Colonial, Eric Wakaonna, Larry Mah, Prevailing Wind, Phillip Proctor, Mya Momiji, SurveysXpress, QuickFlight Miles, and Reada Dailey in their hard work and help to make this book possible.

Second Life research and filming locations included: Skybox Casino and Mall, The Ricardo Group Office Complex, Archebooks Bookstore, PostNet, Wakaonna Business, various public sandboxes, SL Help Island, and ………the World.

A special heart felt recognition to Carl Post; who has always been there encouraging us all to grow beyond even our own expectations. Carl is not gone but is enjoying a Second Life.

Visit the ArcheBooks Bookstore
Taesot (169,47,117)
in Second Life

How to Use This Book

You've heard about Second Life (SL), read articles about it, and you're curious enough to want to try it. Where do you begin? Looks complicated? It's not, once you get a handle on the basics.

This book is designed to give you the SL essentials quickly and painlessly. Our goal is to take away any apprehension you might be feeling, eliminate the frustration often experienced by the brand new Second Life resident, and make you a veteran player and resident as quickly as possible so you can have fun. After all, that's what Second Life is all about.

You can read this book from cover to cover; or just graze through the tips we offer as "in-world" experts. There are 20 Chapters. Many of the Chapters have practice **Exercises**; there are a bunch of **Tips, Hints and Shortcut Commands** for quick reference, plus **Information** on the Second Life Tools, Tabs, Menus and Things. Spend less than an Hour on each Chapter, or Breeze through a couple of Chapters a day. Design your own approach and become a seasoned resident in a matter of a few days or a maximum of a week. It's that easy.

Make notes in the book and gift one to a friend. When you complete the book, take the Quick Flight Activity Challenge in the Appendix, and if you meet us "in-world" don't forget to say "Hi."

Oh, also browse the **ArcheBooks Publishing** Bookstore in **Taesot (169, 47,117)** where we always have something for everyone. Continually check back with us for additional Books on Second Life.

What is Second Life? In their own words...

WHAT IS SECOND LIFE? : SHOWCASE : BUSINESS & EDUCATION : DEVELOPERS : COMMUNITY : BLOG : SUPPORT

WHAT IS SECOND LIFE?

The World
- Create an Avatar
- Explore
- Meet People
- Own Virtual Land
- Have Fun

The Creations
- Create Anything
- Building
- Scripting

The Marketplace
- Economy
- Economy Graphs
- Economic Statistics
- LindeX Market Data
- Business Opportunities
- Businesses on the Web
- IP Rights

Memberships & Pricing
- Membership Plans
- Land Pricing & Use Fees

FAQs

What is Second Life?

Second Life is a 3-D virtual world entirely built and owned by its residents. Since opening to the public in 2003, it has grown explosively and today is inhabited by a total of 4,751,091 people from around the globe.

- From the moment you enter the World you'll discover a vast digital continent, teeming with people, entertainment, experiences and opportunity. Once you've explored a bit, perhaps you'll find a perfect parcel of land to build your house or business.

- You'll also be surrounded by the Creations of your fellow residents. Because residents retain the rights to their digital creations, they can buy, sell and trade with other residents.

- The Marketplace currently supports millions of US dollars in monthly transactions. This commerce is handled with the in-world unit-of-trade, the Linden dollar, which can be converted to US dollars at several thriving online Linden Dollar exchanges.

Welcome to Second Life. We look forward to seeing you in-world.

A BEGINNER'S GUIDE TO SECOND LIFE®

Your Quick Start Guide to the
Virtual World of Second Life

TABLE OF CONTENTS

CHAPTER 1: MAKING HISTORY
Get a Life... A Second Life

What is everyone talking about?

Your first question was probably "What *is* it?" You heard "3-D virtual world" and "game" in the same sentence and figured a computer-based simulated environment. Your interpretation was that it's a Massively Multiplayer Online Game (MMOG). Then you were patiently told that you are a resident of this world in real time, so you labeled it MMO-RPG (Role-Playing Game) and then added a RTS (Real-Time Strategy). Sure, keep piling on those acronyms. You really won't understand it until you enter this popular new Social Environment yourself and experience first hand what everyone is buzzing about. In the meantime, it is easier to tell you what it is not. This is not objective-based gameplay. It is not combat play (though there are areas that do support combat, it is not the focus). There are no clear winners and losers. The game does not have levels of play and it does not end.

Second Life (**www.secondlife.com**) created by Linden Lab (**www.lindenlab.com**) is not promoted as a "game" Instead the people at Linden Lab truly see it as a 3-D virtual world, and only different from our Earth in that this world is "lived" via the Internet. Second Life opened to the public in 2003, and has been growing explosively ever since. Already millions of people from around the Real World have inhabited it.

Phillip Linden (aka Phillip Rosedale) has expressed that Second Life is passionate about creating a new version of an [Earth] where there is a fundamentally different and better set of capabilities[1] (we're not sure what that means, but it sounds good). He says this means they want SL to be able to reach everyone in the world, to be able to scale to 100s of millions of users and millions of servers, and to remain an open decentralized system in which creativity rules. We're not sure what that means either...but we are sold on Second Life. Our recommendation is that the best way to understand it is to experience it first hand.

Huh, I think I have it. Tell me again

Second life is resident driven and self-evolving. It emphasizes socializing and an in-world virtual economy driven by the sale and purchase of the content created by its members. The closest description of it would be to call Second Life by a subgenre of "Non-combat MMOSG (Massively Multiplayer Online Social Game)."

Second Life is the first of its kind to achieve widespread success including attention from mainstream media, the growing interest from international communities, and multi-national organizations looking to

---

[1]Summary of a SL Forum post 04-07-2006, 03:49 PM by Phillip Linden, CEO/Founder Linden Lab.

expand brand awareness. Think of it as Myspace, YouTube, Amazon, eBay, and Sim City all wrapped up together with Reuters, Toyota, Rockefeller Center, you, me, and VOIP. Pretty crazy, huh?

The SL world is computer-based and appears similar to the real world, with real world rules such as gravity, wind, topography, locomotion, real-time actions, and communication. Communication has been in the form of text typing, but now real-time voice communication is available using VOIP (Voice over Internet Protocol). The push is for Second Life and Real Life (RL) to merge in business, communications, entertainment, and virtually ("really") everything.

About Second Life

Second Life (SL) content is about 90% resident-built. The environment is the creation of Linden Lab (LL) whose name reflects their original address at 333 Linden Street, San Francisco. LL introduced "Linden World" in 2002 which was more like a theme park. They later renamed their development to "Second Life" and opened it to the general public in 2003. While SL is not the first virtual world of its kind, it is a market leader in many ways.

The most unique aspect of Second Life is the fact that the users own the intellectual property of their "in-world" creations. This has allowed users to create products in SL and then later "export" them to another medium and still maintain ownership of that creation. The most noted is **Tringo**, which is recognized as the first real world product created in a virtual world. Tringo blends aspects of puzzle games and bingo. Tringo is now offered on Nintendo Game Boy Advance, ITV, PC, and mobile platforms.

Second Life members are referred to as **residents**. This term was introduced by Linden Lab to give users the feeling of belonging and ownership. Linden Lab continues to give residents as much control over the content in the world as possible, which is evident in the creation tools available and now SL's open source code. SL allows residents to create interface businesses and exchanges. Residents openly trade money, real estate, services, and products. They create objects in-world with primitive shapes (cubes, cylinders, spheres, etc.); upload images, sounds, and animations for a small fee; and have a range of tools to control their environment. There is a robust scripting engine called Linden Script Language (LSL), which residents use to program objects that interact.

The economy within Second Life is dependent on the Linden Dollar (L$) which allows residents to buy and sell the items they have created. The Linden currency can also be traded for US dollars (USD$) via the LindeX service (run by Linden Lab with "controls" restricting volume trades). The economy is closely monitored by LL to insure stabilization of the Linden Dollar. The **sinks** (things that cause L$ to be disposed of) and **sources** (things that introduce L$ into the economy) are managed and publicly reported. LL actively watches the indicators and intervenes to prevent swinging inflation or deflation in the value of the L$.

Residents buy the currency using real credit cards and can cash them in using an official SL exchange rate. More and more residents are claiming income that equals real life income. Residents have also become to claim assets valued at more than a million US dollars mostly stemming from SL real estate dealings. Linden Lab makes its money by selling and charging "tier" fees on the real estate in Second Life. They also take a cut on currency exchanges, receive membership fees, and charge for uploading images, sound, and animations.

The trademark logo chosen for Second Life is a hand (see illustration). It can readily be found throughout SL and RL (Real Life) displayed in different colors and with or without the words "Second Life." The hand symbol, with an inset of what appears to look like an eye, appears in various Linden creations and has been seen on both the sun and the moon. The hand as a symbol is considered important in real life civilizations as well. In many different cultures throughout the ages, the mysterious hand symbol has appeared in paintings and other art forms.

The Teen Connection

Teen Second Life was introduced by LL in early 2005 for kids age 13-17 to develop a parallel world on a Teen specific grid. This was done to prevent teens from entering false information to participate in the **Main Grid** which is strictly reserved for people aged 18 and over. The **Teen Grid** also restricts adult interaction.

Beginning January 1, 2006, the Teen Grid expanded their hours from the Linden Lab office hours to a more realistic 24/7 (24 hours 7 days a week). The Teen Grid is patrolled by Lindens (Linden Lab employees) to insure a safe environment. The teen side has not experienced the same degree of robust growth as the Main Grid.

Teens seem confused about Second Life and often approach it like another combat game. It's not unusual to see weapons and combat gear in full view. Similar to the Main Grid, the residents are in control of the environment's growth and development. When a teen Avatar turns 18 they are transferred with their content and any private islands they own to the Main Grid.

In an attempt to encourage more development and educational programs on the Teen Grid, Linden Lab restricts adult presence on the teen side to Private Islands but the adults have to submit to a background check and the Island has to have visibly posted that adults are present.

Real World Collides with Second Life

SL is experiencing the typical growing pains associated with explosive growth. It is also an open environment which means it can be used by anyone with Internet access. This creates a number of real world problems ranging from the technical (Budgeting of server resources and viral attacks), to moral (Pornography), to legal (copyright infringements, gambling laws, and general lawsuits).

And of course, not all press is good press. Second Life continues to have its share of critics. Overall the press has embraced it. This is illustrated with the impressive number of positive articles on Second Life that have been published by well known news agencies.

Second Life has also been recognized as an educational environment. Perfect for distance learning, computer supported cooperative work, simulations, and corporate training. Allowing individuals to practice skills, try new ideas, and learn from their mistakes. Second Life is already being heralded for its potential to enrich existing curricula and supplement the traditional classroom. Virtual reality gameplay is increasingly being embraced as a vehicle to reach and influence the masses.

Whoever you are, wherever you live, and whatever you do in Real Life doesn't matter here. Your age, physical limitations, socio-economic status, race, language, job skills, and education are only what you make of them. Quoted from the creators of Second Life:

"Your World. Your Imagination."

CHAPTER 2:
QUICKLY UP AND FLYING
Walking and Chewing Gum

Why Second Life?

Ever dream of being someplace far away, being someone else, or looking different then you do? What would it be like in a world where you get to choose who you are, how you look, where you live, and what you do? Does it sound too good to be true? It's here and it's within easy reach through the Internet. Escape with us to the three dimensional virtual world called Second Life (SL).

In SL you get to create yourself and re-create yourself as many times as you want. Sign up free or choose a membership plan. Either way, you receive your own fantasy person, an **Avatar** (your in-world persona). You get to create and develop your Avatar's appearance, personality, and interests. Later, you might even find reasons to have more than one Avatar in Second Life.

SIGN-UP TIPS AND HINTS:

- Don't stress over which membership type to select, it can easily be changed later. Subscribe free just to get started. Add a credit card when initially signing up for a free account and automatically receive some Linden Dollars (your credit card will not be charged).

- Choose your name carefully (this **CANNOT** be changed later, though you can sign up again under another name but you will probably want to keep your first Avatar).

- Pick any body type to start, this you **CAN** change and re-create as many times as you want.

- Download Second Life Software. Make note of the system requirements to make sure your computer can handle it.

Orientation or Experience?

Once you've signed up and downloaded the software, you are now ready to begin. All new Avatars start on **Orientation Island** ("OI") and then have the option to **Teleport** to one of the Mainland welcome areas for exploration or a **Help Island** ("HI"). Help Island's access is restricted to **Mentors**, **Greeters**, **Live Helpers** and some Lindens (employees of Second Life's creator "Linden Lab"). The Orientation approach keeps changing as Linden Lab receives feedback and perfects the experience.

If you have the time, and patience you can easily spend eight hours or more at these Orientation locations preparing for your entrance into Second Life. Or like the rest of us, you can just get out there and start learning by trial and error (which is highly recommended). If you choose the latter, this book is for you. Our goal is to give you the basics you need in order to quickly adapt to SL and look less like a Newbie. Once you acquire the basic knowledge and skills needed for appearance, motion, building, and exploring, you can simply relax and enjoy creating, networking, shopping, and gaming to your hearts content. Then, if you choose to become a more advanced player, you can contribute to Second Life through your own innovative and productive endeavors.

ORIENTATION TIPS AND HINTS:

- Orientation Island is set as your starting point. This Island provides a couple very short Note card tutorials and then offers to teleport you to one of the Orientation Help Islands to further your knowledge. Once you exit these islands, you cannot return unless you sign up a new Avatar. Don't worry; there are other locations we will talk about that will give you the same information (in case you really feel you missed something).

- When you first see your Avatar, move it (see **EXERCISE 1**), other new Avatars will start landing on top of you at this same landing point.

- Don't worry that your clothes look like they might not be loaded yet; and don't worry if you look like everyone else; or as confused as everyone else, you will quickly get over it.

- First thing to do is to start walking and get away from the landing point. Don't worry about bumping into people, everyone does it.

The Obvious Isn't So Obvious

One of the first things you will notice in SL is it is full of things that just aren't obvious. We are going to be talking about a whole lot of the basics in this book and even if what we say seems obvious, if you actually do read everything we write you will find out that there is a lot of things that aren't so obvious that you will be picking up in these lessons.

If you have a friend who is also new to SL, it helps to share your new found wisdom (and shortcuts). Sharing information is the quickest way to getting up and running (flying in this case). Even if you have been in SL for awhile, some of the basics may have eluded you. We may just have the information here you are looking for.

Believe it or not, the first obviously counterintuitive thing you'll face is just moving your Avatar around. The default view has a camera looking past your Avatar from behind. That's called a third person mode. Later we will explain how to move the camera around to even look at your avatar from the front. Right now work through this first of many exercises to come.

Note: When the words *Click* or *Select* are used, it is the same as being instructed to *Left-click* using your mouse. Alternate commands are designated by parenthesis ( ).

EXERCISE 1: MOVEMENT

Practice using the arrow key (↑) on your keyboard and pointing your mouse in the direction you want your Avatar to walk.

BASIC WALKING

♦ Move your mouse to the top of the screen above your Avatar's head. Notice that your Avatar looks up.

♦ Move your mouse down to the ground and notice your Avatar looks down.

♦ Use your up arrow key (↑) on your keyboard and your Avatar walks forward.

♦ Try (←) and your Avatar turns to the left. Use (→) and the Avatar turns to the right. Press (↓) and your Avatar walks backwards. Try the different arrow keys to see what happens. Also, try the page up and page down key. Now you're jumping and squatting. See, it's that easy.

ADVANCED WALKING

♦ **Mouselook:** If you have one, roll forward the wheel located on your mouse; or if you don't have a wheel mouse, press the "m" (same as M) key and the view on your screen changes to *mouselook*. Make sure **Chat** is closed (use the esc key or toggle **Chat** by pressing the **Chat** button) when you type a single letter command like "M". You are now looking at the world through the eyes of your Avatar. The *mouselook* makes it a lot easier to move your Avatar and maneuver through tight spaces. It will also make flying easier.

◆ When in *mouselook* look for a cursor symbol in the middle of your screen. Using your mouse, point that symbol to where you want to look, walk, or fly.

◆ When walking or flying, keep the cursor at the level of the horizon. This gives you the best control over your direction and your location between the ground and sky.

◆ Keep your *mouselook* cursor in the center of your screen and press the forward arrow key (↑).

◆ Now move your *mouselook* cursor to where you want your Avatar to look or to move when pressing the arrow key (↑).

FLYING

◆ Stay in *mouselook* and *left-click* the Blue "**Fly**" button on the bottom of your screen.

◆ Move your *mouselook* cursor slightly up from the horizon while pressing the forward arrow (↑).

◆ Move your *mouselook* cursor back to the horizon. Then move the cursor right (or left) in the direction you want to move. At the same time press your forward arrow (↑) on the keyboard.

◆ Now you are flying. Practice flying around.

LANDING

◆ Point your *mouselook* cursor symbol to the ground while pressing the forward arrow key (↑).

◆ Once you are close to the ground, *left-click* the "**Stop Flying**" button at the bottom of your screen and your Avatar will land.

◆ Practice letting up on your arrow key (↑) as you get close to the ground for a smoother landing.

◆ Another way to land is to use your **Page Down** key. Once you are at the spot you want to land, hold **Page Down** and it will give you a solid landing keeping you balanced and on your feet. Keep your *mouselook* at the horizon or come out of *mouselook* for the landing.

You'll soon get the hang of it...we all do.

Sometimes Everyone Is Klutzy

If you bump or accidentally shove someone, remember to apologize. It happens to all of us, and saying "sorry" isn't ever really out of place. Sometimes you'll find yourself in a crowd or a confined space where you can't maneuver well so it is not uncommon to walk into things and people. This happens a lot when you first arrive in a location and everything around you hasn't yet **rezzed** (gained full resolution, i.e. appeared). Just go slow while you are trying to get the hang of it.

Besides walking you can actually set your Avatar to run. Practically nobody does this but Newbies, because it's really not faster than walking and the effect looks pretty silly. But if you want to, just *left-click* **World** on the Menu Bar and select **Always Run** (Ctrl-R). Turn it off the same way.

Flying, of course is the fastest way to go. Wow, wouldn't that be great if we could fly like this in real life? It is a whole lot more fun then walking. As soon as you start flying, you will notice that graceful landings take a little practice. The tricks to it are part of the Exercise and the Tips in this Chapter.

SHORTCUT COMMANDS:

Mouselook Toggle*	M (or roll mouse wheel)
Exit *Mouselook***	esc
Fly Toggle**	Home
Fly**	Page Up + ↑
Stop Flying**	Page Down
Always Run	Ctrl-R

*Make sure Chat bar is closed when typing a single letter command.

**Press designated key on your keyboard

WALKING AND FLYING TIPS AND HINTS:

- Press LIGHTLY on the arrow key. Common mistake is to be heavy handed and over fly your target, fly into things, or walk into people.

- Touch the "escape" (esc) key or press "M" on your keyboard to turn off *mouselook*. OR *rollback* the wheel on your mouse if you have one. When you can see your Avatar, you are no longer in *mouselook*.

- Point your *mouselook* cursor straight up and you will look in that direction.

- Point your *mouselook* cursor and Press the arrow key (↑) or Press your "Page Up" key and you are walking or flying in the direction of your cursor.

- Always remember, you will look, fly, or walk in the direction of your *mouselook* cursor.

- You can release *mouselook* at any time and re-enable it at any time; even in mid movement. Just make sure that your **Chat** (esc) is closed if you use the "M" to toggle.

- If your movements feel too fast, **hold the space-bar down** on your keyboard, it will slow you down until you feel more control over walking and flying.

- *Left-click* is also used for the Menu Bar at the top of your screen and the Button Bar at the bottom.

- Generally speaking, *left-click* is used simply to select and the *right-click* usually is used to open for more information within Second Life (Windows, Pie Menus, etc.).

You're Basically There

You now have the basics of movement under control, but you are still on Orientation Island. You can follow the path and read all of the detailed instructions or just do the minimum requirements to get to the Exit. Since Linden Lab keeps changing the Orientation experience, we can't direct you exactly how to get out, but the faster you can, the faster you can start living.

Typically, from Orientation you are transferred to a Help Island. Since they transport you there as a Newbie, take advantage of the environment for some of the following chapters. We recommend you continue breezing through a couple of these basics and then we will help you step into the real Second Life. There's plenty more to know, you can tell that just by the number of Chapters in this Book. Trust me, the book will get you through your Newbie period a lot faster then trying to go through all of those learning stations.

CHAPTER 3:
GATHERING INFORMATION
What you Don't Know

Notecard Information

Okay, so you believe you might be missing something if you don't explore everything on these Orientation and Help Islands. The information offered can overwhelm you. Some players get frustrated by trying to absorb everything in Orientation and Help and they don't return to SL; or they let too much time pass before they return and are frustrated having to review the same information and still don't fully grasp what SL is all about. Since you can't begin to actually live and experience SL until you understand the basics, let's compromise with the following exercise.

EXERCISE 2: ORIENTATION AND NOTES

Satisfy your curiosity by going to the required stations in Orientation and then get over to the Help Island as quickly as you can. The Second Life stations will offer up information. Since there is no quiz required to get off these Islands, go ahead and follow the steps below, learn something from the process, and satisfy your curiosity at the same time.

- ◆ Go ahead and visit some of the locations on the Help Island. *Left-click* on where you see the green SL hand and you're offered a **Note**. If it is a topic you want to reference later, go ahead and *click* the button to "**Keep**."

- ◆ In fact *click* on the same station a second time. This time when the Note appears *click* the button "**Discard**". The Note is no longer saved for future reference.

- ◆ Now *click* on that same station a third time. Instead of clicking a button, go ahead and *click* the "**X**" on the upper right hand corner. Got rid of it you think? You're wrong. If you don't "**Discard**" a Note, it automatically is saved for you.

- ◆ Now find the Notes you saved. *Click* on the **Inventory** (Ctrl-I) button in the right hand bottom corner of your screen. In your inventory list is a folder called **Notecards**. *Double left-click* on the folder and locate the two Notes you just saved. Go ahead *double left-click* a Note or *right-click, select* **Open** and prove to yourself it is the same one you saved.

- ◆ Now "**X**" and the Note will go back into **Inventory**.

- ◆ Go back to one of the Notes in your **Notecards** Folder and *right-click* and *select* "**Properties**". You can see the properties of any saved inventory item this way. It will tell you the name, description, creator, owner, and list the permissions you were given. Permissions include whether you can share, modify, transfer, etc.

◆ Close "**Properties**" and *right-click* one of the duplicate Notes and *select* "**Delete**". Now that Note is gone.

◆ Now look in the folder labeled as "**Trash**" in your **Inventory**. That's where your deleted Note landed.

Go ahead and *click* on all the Orientation and Help Stations if you want and grab the Notes. However, you'll probably never get around to reading them once you have a life (Second Life that is).

NOTECARD TIPS AND HINTS:

• Most Newbies take anything that is offered to them FREE. All those Objects, Notes, Landmarks, Clothes, Textures, Scripts, Friendships, etc. are stored in your **Inventory** (Ctrl-I).

• Over time it is hard to find things in your Inventory when you need it. You will probably even lose track of what's in there. We will talk about **Inventory** and Inventory Management later, but for now, think about how you might use something before you take it.

• Remember, when you are offered a Note, if you don't click "**Discard**" it is automatically saved to your **Inventory**. That file then will fill up fast with unwanted Notes.

• Some Notes can be modified if you want to change information on it— don't know why you would. Some Notes are locked and may not let you even copy or transfer them. *Right-click* any item in your inventory file and you are presented with a "**Properties**" option that lists the permissions you are given for the item.

• You can create your own Notecard when you are in **Inventory**. *Right-click* on a folder or *left-click* on "**Create**" to open a menu, and then select **New Note**. You can also **Create New Gestures, Scripts, Folder, Clothes, and Body Parts**. You don't need this knowledge now; we will talk about it later when you are ready to create your own objects "in-world".

Learn by Doing

You have just enough information about how Notes work for now. The best way you are going to learn is by **doing**. Plus, you will have more fun than trying to read all those instructional cards. We're going to get you talking to residents. They are the best source for information and advice. You are going to learn how to *right-click* on an Avatar to find their SL age. The oldest age possible would date back to 2004.

As you work through these exercises, keep moving through Orientation to where it ends so you can exit. The Orientation experience keeps being redesigned, so we can't tell you exactly how to get out of there. In the meantime, follow these exercises, practice your walking and flying and you make your way through the SL Maze of lessons on your way to finding the **EXIT**.

Right Click for More Information

This section can be performed almost anywhere. Since Orientation Island does not offer much information on its objects, keep following the walking path and find the "Exit" platform with instructions for Teleporting to a Help or Welcome location. Now onto the next exercise, SL tools offer a lot of information.

By now you should have noticed the menu bar at the top of your screen and the buttons at the bottom of your screen. In addition, you can learn more about all of the people and objects you see by using the *right-click* on your mouse. Try it, *right-click* on an object or a person and a **Pie Menu** appears. *Click* on the menu options and additional tabs and information are presented to you. A couple more things follow that I recommend you learn in this chapter before leaving Orientation.

EXERCISE 3: RIGHT CLICK OBJECTS AND PEOPLE

Right-click an object or Avatar in Second Life and you can see information about it.

- ◆ Go ahead and position your cursor on any Avatar and *right-click*. A Pie Menu will open, *click* on "**Profile**" and an information window will open on your screen.

- ◆ This window displays the name of the Avatar. It also states the Avatar's birth date and whether the Avatar has "**Payment Info On File**" which means a free account or "**Payment Info In Use**" identifying it as a paid membership account. Free accounts with NO credit card information listed will state "**No Payment Info On File**" for that Avatar. We will talk more about this window and the tabs once you leave Help Island. For now, just be aware of it. You will want to *right-click* on the different people you meet.

- ◆ Now *right-click* on a couple of different objects. A pie menu will appear. Depending on the item, different options will be offered. The "**Edit**" option provides the information on Objects. When you explore in Second Life, you will find this to be helpful.

- ◆ *Right-click* the land you are standing on. It will also offer up information. *Right-click* anything and everything around you. *Right-click* is a powerful information producing tool.

- ◆ You probably even tried right clicking on your own Avatar. A different information pie menu appears. This menu allows you to change your **Appearance**, manage your **Friends**, **Groups**, and **Profile**.

RIGHT CLICK TIPS AND HINTS:

- You can't *right-click* in *mouselook*. Exit *mouselook* (use the escape key, M, or rollback the mouse) to use this function.

- When you *right-click* people (select profile) they don't know you are doing so. The Profile page displays the age information reflects the experience level of the resident. When people *right-click* on your Avatar, they will know immediately that you are new.

- The Profile page displays the avatar's name. If you meet someone with the last name "Linden", they are an employee of Linden Lab.

- *Right-click* objects in Second Life for an options pie menu. The options displayed are set by both the creator and/or the owner. The object's menu may offer you to **Sit Here**, **Wear**, **Buy**, **Take**, or **Take Copy**, etc. You can also report the object for abuse. More on all of this later.

- You will soon be creating your own objects and some of your menu options will be automatically set and other available options you set the Permissions.

- *Right-click* land information for ownership data, land settings, objects restrictions, etc.

- Check out the *right-click* on your own Avatar but leave everything alone for now. Once you are off Help Island (HI) you will see more options for your **Appearance**.

The fun is just beginning, but you have to get out of these Orientation Island (OI) Areas and into Second Life (SL).

SHORTCUT COMMANDS:

Information on Avatars	*Right-click:* **Profile**
Information on Objects	*Right-click:* **Edit**
Information on Land	*Right-click:* **About Land**
Open Inventory	Ctrl-I
Information on File Item	*Right-click:* **Properties**

Don't Make that Common Newbie Mistake

You might not want to debut into Second Life looking like a cloned Avatar and are now thinking about exploring the "**Appearance**" option that you saw when you *right-clicked* on your Avatar. Try to control the urge. The danger of playing with your clothes and appearance at this point is that we notice Newbies even faster when they try to redesign their clothes and Appearance too soon.

If you're not patient with working on your appearance at this point, and you leave the Orientation Island without perfecting a look, it's obvious you are a Newbie and we will point that out. Once we saw a male newbie on our land walking around naked with only skintight white shorts, an uneven hair application, and nerd glasses. Get the point?

Better to keep your original Avatar body and clothes than to look like a complete idiot. Let's just get you out of Orientation, and you will have a wider range of options available to you for remaking yourself. You will also get ideas from other Avatars you see in Second Life.

CHAPTER 4:
TALK IS CHEAP
Say What?

Let's Talk

Since Orientation consists of new people, and a lot of them, take advantage of this setting by practicing interacting with them first. Look at the menu bar at the top of your screen and the buttons on the bottom of your screen.

Let's concentrate on the blue buttons labeled as **Chat** and **IM (Instant Message)**. In Second Life these are the two main ways you will communicate with other residents. Text **Chat** (Enter key) is similar to holding a conversation with someone you see and may even be looking at, similar to what you do in real life, i.e. anyone nearby can overhear what you say and comment. **An instant message** (Ctrl-T) is more like a telephone conversation. The individual does not have to be anywhere near and you are the only two people on the line. So you see, **IM** is a private channel and **Chat** is a public channel.

Chat allows you to talk to one or more people within close proximity. When you use your Enter key or press the **Say** button to send your text **Chat**, it registers on the screen of any Avatar that is within 20 meters of your Avatar. Residents that are toward the edge of this range will see your chat as a lighter gray.

If you press the **Shout** button instead, it is the equivalent to yelling, so someone up to 100 meters away will receive a copy of your text. That's how it works. Go ahead and try the Chat and IM exercise below.

EXERCISE 4: BASIC CHAT AND MESSAGING

Remember you will meet people from all over the world, awake in different time zones, with a wide variety of interests and reasons for being here. A good part of the fun of SL is just meeting new people and talking.

LET'S CHAT

- ◆ *Left-click* the blue **Chat** button (Enter key) and a typing window will appear.

- ◆ Start a public conversation with any Avatar. Go ahead just type "hi" and hit the "Enter" key or *click* **Say**. It helps to type the first name of who you are addressing so they know you are trying to talk to them. Their name appears over their head.

- ◆ Talk to a couple of different people for a few minutes. Ask them if they know how to get out of Orientation or if they have heard of any interesting places to go. Ask them if they know where any of the free stuff is. Ask them how to do something. Ask them where the Exit is. Just ask questions to start some conversation.

♦ Now *left-click* on the "**History**" button (Ctrl-H) on the bottom of your screen. You can see it when **Chat** is open for typing. You can now reference any conversation you or anyone near you had. Notice that other conversations will appear on your screen and you are actually overhearing conversations that you are not even participating in.

LET'S MESSAGE

There are different ways to begin Instant Message (**IM**). You will practice two of them here. Remember, use **IM** for private conversations.

♦ *Right-click* on an Avatar that you can see. Doesn't matter how far they are from you. A pie menu will open; *select* the **Send IM** Option. And type "Hi". Note the Avatars name is on the tab in the IM typing window.

♦ Pick another Avatar and *right-click* again. This time *left-click* and select the **Profile** option. At the bottom of the **Profile** screen there is an **Instant Message** button. *Click* on the button and start messaging. Say something...anything.

♦ Go ahead, *right-click* another Avatar and start another Instant Message. Then at the same time use your open **Chat** and start a conversation. Ask them if they know where the Exit is. The idea is to talk (by typing).

♦ Now see how many conversations you can keep going at the same time. If your **IM** is open in conversation, the Avatar's name tab will start blinking when you receive a reply from that respective Avatar. Click on it to make it stop blinking. If you reply always make sure you type your response in the right **IM** space for that Avatar.

CHAT AND IM TIPS AND HINTS:

- You can have more than one **IM** conversation at the same time.

- Be careful. Make sure you are in **IM** (Ctrl-T) when messaging. It's very easy to forget and respond to an **IM** through **Chat** and everyone around you will see what you typed.

- When your **IM** window is open, the name tab blinks when a reply is received. You may miss the message in your lower left screen with the **IM** window open.

- When you **IM**, your Avatar does not perform the typing animation or relay a typing sound (which you do have in **Chat** mode)

- Note that **IM** replies will create a blink to signal you of a new message if you are busy doing something else on your computer. The Second Life tab in your tray will start to blink telling you there is some kind of message waiting for you.

- The **History** of your conversations are captured in **IM** and **Chat** so you can go back and re-read it.

- **Chat** and **IM** history is erased when you leave Second Life. When you re-enter SL, **Chat** and **IM** will start recording again.

- **IM** messages start with IM: when they appear in the lower left corner of your screen.

- You can view and read your **IM** messages in **IM** with the history. Or you can just read them on your screen and choose to ignore them. All messages eventually just disappear from your screen.

- Normal chat has a range of 20 meters. Residents that are toward the edge of this range will see your chat as a lighter gray.

- An Avatar name is often printed over the character's head (though they can shut that feature off or change the display properties). If you don't see their name, just *right-click* on them and their **Profile** pane will appear displaying their name.

- *Right-click* an Avatar and select "**Send IM**" to begin an **Instant Message** session with them.

- You can **IM** someone who is not online. You can find them through **Search** (Ctrl-F) or your **Friends** (Ctrl-Shift-F) list. You will receive a message from SL saying the information will be stored for them.

[13:55] Second Life: User not online - message will be stored and delivered later.

CHAT AND IM TIPS AND HINTS: (Cont.)

- The **IM** is sent to their email account unless they turned the forward feature off. Either way the message will be displayed on their screen and in their **IM** file when they sign back on.

- Second Life (SL) time is noted in your upper right hand corner of your screen. It is the same as Pacific Standard Time (PST) because that's where Linden Lab is, the creators are in San Francisco, California. All conversation is time stamped as military time (14:00 is 2:00 PM) and it is considered to be SL time.

- If you hit Enter when the chat line is blank it will close.

- The only way out of Orientation Island is by "EXIT," an area at the end of the Orientation path marked clearly with an "EXIT" sign. Once your Avatar leaves, that Avatar cannot return here. Don't worry; there are other locations for information and tutorials available once you leave OI and HI.

SHORTCUT COMMANDS:

Chat	Enter/Return Key
Hide Chat	Esc
Chat History*	Ctrl-H
Instant Message (Talk)*	Ctrl-T
Say	Enter
Shout	Ctrl-Enter
No Hand movement	"/" then type message

These commands turn the function on and off.

Walk Around and Talk About

Don't worry about embarrassing yourself; they don't know you, and you may never meet them again. Plus if you do, they won't even recognize you since you will have probably remade yourself at least 5 or 10 times over.

Finish making your way looking around the Orientation area to satisfy your curiosity. Pick up some free stuff, and then it is really time for you to move on. The easiest way to leave is by **Teleporting**. If you close the Second Life program before leaving Orientation, you will automatically appear again and again in Orientation until you actually leave and establish your "home" someplace else.

INFORMATION:
CHAT, MESSAGE, MUTE, AND MORE

CHAT (Ctrl-T): Opens a type bar for typing messages in order to speak to the Avatars around you. This is a public relay channel and the messages appear in your lower left side of your screen. Always prevue your lower left hand screen when something appears. Avatars may be trying to chat with you.

When you **Chat,** your Avatar will begin a typing animation that includes sound. This signals others that you are about to speak. You can suppress the typing sound and animation by starting your line of chat text with a forward slash '/' character.

HISTORY (Ctrl-H): All **Chat** messages are recorded for the SL session. Chat History will identify the time and source on the line before the message. The Chat History with an object called "New Car" looks like this:

> [12:01] Tara Anna: hi car, where are you from?
> [12:02] New Car: why do you want to know?

INSTANT MESSAGES (IMs): They appear in the lower left of your screen but will have **IM** at the beginning of the message.

An **IM** recording with Carl Post will look like this:

> [12:01] IM: Tara Anna: hi Carl, where are you from?
> [12:02] IM: Carl Post: hi Tara, New York

Objects can also be made to chat or message. Sometimes objects will chat through the public channels and may relay their message when you touch them or go near them. This is a "scripted" (which means programmed) object and it may also be set to use a different channels (other than **Chat** and **IM**) for relaying a message. If it is a private channel the message will appear in a color other than white. This type of private messaging is often done so the messages don't congest the conversation traffic of the non-involved Avatar (which can be irritating).

If you respond to the relay of the private Instant Message using the public **Chat** system, your part of the conversation becomes publicly displayed on the screen and the object will not receive your reply.

INFORMATION:
CHAT, MESSAGE, MUTE, AND MORE (Cont.)

MUTE: You have the option to silence the talking of an object or an Avatar. This allows you to eliminate that person's or object's **Chat** or **IM** from your screen. You cannot mute sounds.

An object may instruct you through a message, help request, or a Note-card to use their channel. If that is the case, you will be instructed to respond using a "/" with a channel number. Then, on the same line type your response. (e.g. '/100blue' may be your reply to turn an object called "blue"). Now we are getting ahead of ourselves. You'll be instructed about the channel when you meet an object that requires it.

Voice It Next

This Chapter was about basic communication. There are a number of reasons people come to Second Life. It may be that you are attracted to the Social side of the virtual world. No matter your motivation, you do need to know how to communicate. If you can't communicate, you can't get help, and you will need help at some point and want to find it. We all do. Second Life is very communications-centric. Here we only talk about the basic text approach offered with **Chat** and **IM**, and with that there was a lot to say.

Voice chat is also available and growing in popularity. It's still too new to comment on it at this point for a Newbie. There are so many other things you really need to learn first. So let's move along.

CHAPTER 5:
LET'S GET OUT OF HERE
Search and You Shall Find

Getting off Orientation Island

Trust me, if you've followed the instructions so far, you are ready to leave the Orientation and Help Islands. The easiest way to get out of the Help Island is to **Teleport** (TP) to another Second Life location. Now you need to decide on where you want to go. You have so many options like shopping, gambling, building, working, playing, or just exploring. Not to depress you, but remember you still look and act like a Newbie, you don't have any money, and where in the world should you go? Keep reading, we will get you established faster if you follow our lead.

Let's start by exploring **Search** and taking advantage of getting more of the Free stuff out there. The **Search** button at the bottom of your screen is your shortcut to everything that is happening in-world. With this tool you can easily find the **Popular Places**, interesting **Groups** to join, deals on **Land**, **Shopping Malls, Training Programs, Current Activities,** and a whole lot more. Here is a run-through of the tabs available on the Search window.

INFORMATION: SEARCH (Ctrl-F)

All	Classifieds	Events	Popular Places	Land Sales	Places	People	Groups

Searching (Ctrl-F) is always fun. You never know what you will find. This is a very dynamic world, so expect things to change daily.

ALL: This is a search query across all tabs and categories. The Symbol by each result will indicate the type of listing (classified, events, places, people, and groups). **Search** by key words.

CLASSIFIEDS: The advertiser chooses the amount to pay for one week of advertising. The higher the amount paid the higher the listing is in the Results.

EVENTS: Free Advertising for special events. Event time for the listing is a 3 hours maximum. You can review past and future events.

INFORMATION: SEARCH (Cont.)

POPULAR PLACES: Top 20 high traffic locations. List updated daily. Traffic count is the sum total of time residents spent on a property (**About Land** lists the previous day traffic when you *right-click* on the plot).

LAND SALES: Lists land that is for sale and land that is available at auction.

PLACES: Land name, classification, and listing as set and defined by the Land Owner.

PEOPLE: Search for an Avatar's **Profile** by their SL name.

GROUPS: Search for a Group by name (Group must choose this option to include their name for **Search**).

Search: Used for keyword or exact name searches.

Teleport: When you select from the Search list, details appear in the window on the right. If you want to visit that location, press the Teleport button and you are sent directly there.

Treasure Hunt

It's time to take that big step toward living a Second Life. As you can tell by just reading about the Search Tool and the categories of things to do, places to go, and people to meet. This exercise is your first exposure to serious exploring and searching. You still have a lot more things to learn and practice but we promise some fun in the process. Let the games begin.

EXERCISE 5: LET'S START LIVING

Since you still look like a Newbie and you probably don't have any money (or much money) we recommend you teleport to a Mall or a Freebie Warehouse to pick up a variety of **Free Stuff**.

♦ *Left-click* the blue **Search** button at the bottom of your screen (or Shift-F). This opens the Search Window.

♦ *Left-click* **Places** and type in "Free Stuff." An assorted list of places that match the search words "free stuff" will appear. *Left-click* on any line in the list and on the right side of the window a complete description of the place will appear.

♦ Find a location advertising 100s, 1,000s or even 5,000 Free Stuff that catches your interest. Don't spend a lot of time deciding; remember you are still on Orientation Island. If we don't like what you find when you teleport to the selected location, you can re-open **Search** and easily pick another location and you are out of there.

♦ Once you decide on a location to explore, *left-click*, "**Teleport**" and off you go.

♦ When you get to your destination walk around and try to find the Free Stuff. Sometimes it is difficult to find. If it is, then pick another location in your **Search** list and try again.

♦ When you find Free Stuff of interest, *Right-click* the object and select **Buy** or **Open** to see the contents being offered and the permissions that come with it. Permissions include what you can do as the new owner (**copy, modify, transfer**). Select **Buy**, if available, and it will list the contents of the object and the price, which may be L$0. If you like what you see, then **Buy**.

♦ Once you complete the **Buy** process, the items will be found in your **Inventory**. Generally under the folder titled "**Objects**."

♦ Try to find an assortment of objects. These objects may have contents consisting of scripts, textures, clothes, gadgets, buildings, etc. Acquire them for the next exercise.

♦ Keep looking and enjoy the wonders of SL shopping.

You have now officially entered into your new life. Congratulations!

SEARCH TIPS AND HINTS:

• When you **Teleport** to your location through the **Search** tool, a red beam will mark the coordinates of the resulting Search location. You will notice this after your **Teleport** is complete.

• You might land on a teleport pad that is designated by the landowner, but not the store owner. The teleport pad might be located in the middle of the mall, in front of a directory, or outside the business noted in your search. Follow the red beam (a red arrow will appear on your screen that will point in the direction to look in case you are not facing it). This will help you find your search location.

• Sometimes the grid (reference to Second Life computer servers) has problems with the teleport. Be patient, or try another search location in the meantime. If the area you want to enter is already overpopulated at the moment, then the teleport may redirect you or abort the process. Just try again later.

SEARCH TIPS AND HINTS: (Cont.)

- If you land somewhere and it seems dark, the area might be set for night or sunset. All you need to do is *left-click* **World** in the menu bar, *left-click* "**Force the Sun**" and choose **Noon** (same as Ctrl-Shift-Y). Now you have some daylight so you can see.

- Now look around and *Right-click* Objects for information about them. It will also indicate whether you need to buy or you can just **Take** or **Take Copy** of the Object. Sometimes the "Buy" price is "L$0", so don't be afraid to click on buy to see the price. You can still decide not to **Buy** the object when the window showing the contents and price appears.

- Everything you select to **Buy**, **Take**, or **Take Copy** still ends up in the same place in your **Inventory**. Physical items or items that are boxed can be found under the **Inventory** folder "**Objects**". If you are given a Note it is in **Notecards**. Landmarks are in **Landmarks**.

- Objects, Scripts, Notes, Textures, and even Landmarks can be placed in a box to be sold or transferred to you. These items then can be found in the folder **Objects**. These items will then need to be opened. You will do that in the next exercise.

- In **Search**, when you combine the word, or use a space. "Sand Box" and "Sandbox" it will produce different results. The word or combination of words in Search has to match exactly. Use as few words as possible when searching. Partial words sometimes can work better.

- When you **Teleport** to a location from a Search list, the list closes upon arrival. Open **Search** again and the last search set is still available on each tab.

- Events are held by Residents at all hours of the day and night. Remember that the times listed in the Events window are based on (SLT) in-world time which is the same as Pacific Standard Time (PST).

- The present in-world time can always be found at the top of your screen for reference.

```
┌─────────────────────────────────────────────────┐
│ SHORTCUT COMMANDS:                                │
│                                                   │
│ Search (Find)          Ctrl-F                     │
│ Noon                   Ctrl-Shift-Y               │
│ Sunset                 Ctrl-Shift-N               │
└─────────────────────────────────────────────────┘
```

No Stopping Now

Don't stop here and don't get side-tracked in your **Search**. There is plenty more to learn, see, and do. Not only will you be able to find a bunch of fun Free Stuff, but we will show you how to work on your appearance, find easy ways to shop (for anything—bodies, clothes, weapons, vehicles and more), use public sandboxes for building, buy land, and find those groups and activities that interest you. Plus lots more! When you finish this book, you will be intrigued by the depth and breadth of Second Life.

EXPLORE: SEARCHES TO TRY OUT

If you want to take a break and do some more exploring, try out some of these **Search** Words for fun. For now stick to the Places Tab, later we will explore the other categories. Also, look in the Appendix of this book for a list of more places to Explore in SL. The Region and Associated Coordinates are listed and can be filled into "**Map**" that can be found on your Button Bar.

Free Stuff: Find Free Samples

Sandbox: Public Location for Building

Casino: Gambling Available

Mall: Shopping Area

Combat: Supporting Weapons and Combat

Weapons: Products of Destruction

Camping: Paid to sit on land to increase Traffic

Money Tree: Some L$ for New Residents

Club: Discos, Casinos, Bars, Private Clubs

Beach: Swimwear, boats, pools, Ocean activities

Museum: Traditional, Educational. Art

Library: Traditional, SL related, etc.

Boats: Yachts, live aboard, rentals, slips

Park: Amusement, Animal, Recreational

CHAPTER 6:
STUFF AND MORE STUFF
Don't Be a Pack Rat

Unpack and Stay Awhile

Let's unpack the free stuff and see how successful you were in your hunt. Hopefully you were able to visit a number of places and picked up a wide assortment of things. Now your job is to find a public area ("Sandbox") where you can comfortably investigate your spoils. This will also be a good time to learn basic **Inventory Management** and control. No time like the present to start organizing the stuff.

EXERCISE 6: FIND A SANDBOX AND UNPACK

At this point you don't own land and you don't have a place to call your own. So the best place to go next is a public **Sandbox**. They are great places to unpack inventory, work on your appearance, and try your hand at building things. Let's go.

- *Left-click* **Search** (or Ctrl-F); *Left-click* **Places**; and type "Sandbox".

- Click on one and select **Teleport**. When you get there, try and find some space that gives you elbow room to work. If this Sandbox doesn't feel right, try another. You will eventually have one or two locations where you feel comfortable working.

- If you like the Sandbox, then save it as a **Landmark** so you can find it easily again. In the menu bar *left-click* **World**; then *left-click* "**Create Landmark Here.**" A Landmark request window will open. If you click "**X**" (or Ctrl-W) it will automatically Save to your **Inventory** folder "**Landmarks**" so you can reference it for a **Teleport** in the future.

- Note the rules of the Sandbox. Some sandboxes allow scripts and weapons. Some won't. Most Sandboxes will wipe their land clean at a certain hour. Be aware of that time. The Sandbox will list rules in their Search display as well as post them somewhere on the Land. So look for it. You can be banned from land if you don't follow the rules.

- Once you find a work area in the Sandbox *left-click* your **Inventory** button (Ctrl-I) to gain access to your Inventory files. Take out the first item you have in the file folder "**Objects**". *Left-click* the item, *hold* it and *drag* it out of your **Inventory** to the ground.

- Either the item or a box will "rez" (the term means to "appear") and you can then *right-click* the box, *left-click* "**Open**" and *left-click* "**Copy Inventory**" to get to the item(s). Try it.

- The box's content is now either copied or moved into its own folder identified by the Object's Name.

♦ Your box is still on the ground. You can now *right-click* and find "**Delete**" in the Pie Menu (or *right-click* and press your **delete** key). If you "**Take**" the box, you end up cluttering your **Inventory**.

♦ Try unpacking another box. Then just *drag* an unpacked object from your **Objects** folder in **Inventory**.

Now you have the hang of it. If you decide to leave the Sandbox, please clean-up after yourself. If you leave the items they will automatically be returned to your **Inventory Lost and Found** folder. Deal with these items now or deal with them later.

SOME OBJECT TIPS AND HINTS:

• New Avatars often make the mistake of trying to "**wear**" an object before unpacking it. First *drag* the object onto the floor and *right-click* to open the Pie Menu, and then select the **Open** option. Then "**Copy to Inventory**" the Contents before you *select* **Wear** (*right-click* the **Inventory** file(s) to **Wear**).

• Selecting an Object's **Edit** option opens the **Build** pane with the **Edit** tool pre-selected and the **General Tab** open. If the **General Tab** doesn't fill with information on the first try, *right-click* the object again to force fill it. If it still doesn't seem to want to fill, look at your setting in **Tools** (top Menu Bar) and make sure **Select Only My Objects** is NOT checked.

• If the **Build** pane is blocking your view, *left-click* the top of the pane, *hold* and *drag* it anywhere on your screen to get it out of your way.

• The **General Tab** in the **Build** Tool Box reflects the **Prim Count** of the Object. **Prims** are important to tally since land has a maximum number of Prims it can manage. Don't worry about Prims for now since you don't own land or rent space, we will cover them in the **Build** Exercises later. Just be aware of it for now.

• The **Build** Button opens the Tool Box with the **Create** tool selected. When you **Create** the Object you hold all of the Permissions as the Creator.

• When you *right-click* an object and are able to *select* **Buy**, **Take**, or **Copy** the Creator has allowed the ownership to be passed to you. The item has to pass through your **Inventory** before you are recognized as the owner.

SOME OBJECT TIPS AND HINTS: (Cont.)

- If you lose an Object or leave it in a Sandbox, it will eventually be returned to your **Lost and Found** Folder. Some land owners set their land to automatically return Objects that don't belong to them or members of their Group. Other landowners don't even allow you to place Objects from your **Inventory** or limit the time you have to "show" an Object. Prims count toward the Land's Prim Limit.

- Don't Litter, always clean up after yourself.

Your Inventory is Your Closet of Stuff

The Objects that you unpacked are now in **Inventory** folders. It's time to understand how **Inventory** is structured and to look at some of the objects. Just opening ("rezzing") the objects you collected free can be a learning experience. After you understand the **Edit** function you will have a better appreciation for the details and ingenuity that contributes to a creation. Objects can be set as "physical", and respond to gravity, wind, and weather, just like in real life. An object can be static (just sit there and look good) and other objects are dynamic (they can move, talk, and even change with use).

As you unpack and try out some of your collected inventory, you will soon notice that exploring objects can be fascinating. Some objects can move, talk, respond to you, and follow you. You can link objects, stretch them, resize them, change their textures and colors, and add scripts for dynamic effects.

INVENTORY TIPS AND HINTS:

- You can *drag* files from one folder to another to help you rearrange and organize your **Inventory**.

- If you leave an object on a person's property, in a sandbox, or you lose an object, it will be returned and the object can be found in your **Lost and Found** Folder.

- In **Inventory** you can use a "close all folders" command (**File: Close All Folders**). Then, when you use **Filters** all the folders will open.

- **Library** files can be copied into **Inventory**. They cannot be moved. If you choose a *right-click* Option to "**Wear**" something, the file will automatically transfer to your **Inventory** into the same respective folder assigned in **Library** (as it appears on your Avatar).

- **Inventory** files and folders work like your computer files and folders. *Left-click* opens files and folders in **Inventory**.

- You don't become a designated owner of an item unless you create it or have permission to bring it into your **Inventory**.

- You can move files into different **Inventory** folders, even folders designated for a different file type.

- You can set up your own folders and sub folders. You can add sub folders to SL **Inventory** folders (not **Library** folders).

- When you use **Create**, no matter what folder is highlighted, the item will be created in its own designated folder only. Then you can move it.

INVENTORY TIPS AND HINTS: (Cont.)

- **Library** folders and files cannot be removed or moved around.

- *Right-click* shows options available for the file or folder.

- **Library** folders have no *right-click* options.

- *Right-click* a file, select **Properties** for a quick summary of the Item's permissions and some **General Tab** information without having to take it out of **Inventory**.

- Use the **library** files after you copy and paste them into your **Inventory**. It's less confusing.

- You have to be an owner to store items in your **Inventory**. Only **Library** has your non-owner items given to you by Linden Lab.

The Library is Always There

Library files are fun to explore. Explore these files and become familiar with what Linden Lab has provided. These items are useful examples for Creating Scripts, Appearance, Sounds, Gestures, and Objects. In them are the original Avatar bodies (male and female) that are offered when signing up for membership. These skins and clothes are easily applied if you want to change your look, or later you can use them to "start over" if you screw up your appearance, or if you want to change the gender of your Avatar.

You don't have to worry about losing **Library** files. They are permanent and can only be used when copied into an Object; Worn or Copied to your **Inventory**.

INFORMATION: INVENTORY (Ctrl-I)

You can move the **Inventory** Window to a different part of your screen by clicking on the top bar where it says "Inventory" and dragging it to where you want it to go. The number of Inventory items is listed in the parentheses ( ) next to the word "Inventory". Only the "need to know right now" commands are listed here and explained below. These tools are used more extensively for managing Inventory.

Inventory Menu Bar

1. **FILE:** *Left-click.* Helpful for quickly finding your files

    New Window: Opens a new window, useful when multi-tasking.

    Show Filters: Nice feature for only seeing file types of interest.
    - ☑ **Always Show Folders:** Sets all folders to show
    - ☑ **Since Logoff:** Narrows searches and sorts.

    Close All Folders: Closes all the files listed into their respective folders.

    Empty Trash: Gets rid of everything you previously deleted that is in "**Trash**".

2. **CREATE:** *Left-click.* Don't need to know this now except "**New Folder**".

    New Folder: Name your own folder.

3. **SORT:** *Left-click.* Be aware it's here.

    By Name: Organizes Inventory files alphabetically by the file name.

    By Date: Organizes Inventory files in descending date order; by the date file was added to Inventory.

    Folders always by Name: Check this so your folders are easily found alphabetically.

4. **FILTERS:** *Left-click.* A helpful tool for narrowing searches with unruly inventory.

    Modify Current: Same as **Show Filters**. Helps narrow a search.

    Reset Current: Defaults to a complete setting showing all files and folders in the window.

Inventory Tabs

There are two **Inventory** Tabs.

All Items   Recent Items

1. **ALL ITEMS:** Contains all of your **Inventory** Folders and Files.

2. **RECENT ITEMS:** Reflects additions to your Inventory.
   This tab is cleared when you exit SL.

FOLDER: SL assigned folders (🗀 display with a unique icon inserted into the folder icon); *Left-click* to Open. *Right-click* for Options

> **Standard Options* include: Create New Folder, New Script, New Note, New Gesture, New Clothes** and **New Body Parts**

> **Other Options*: Rename, Copy, Paste, Delete, Add to Outfit, Replace Outfit, Take Off Items,** and **IM All Contacts In Folder**.

FILE: The icon in front of the file name identifies file type; *Left-click* to Open. *Right-click* for Options

> **Standard Options* include: Open, Properties, Rename, Copy Asset UUID, Copy** (Ctrl-C), **Paste** (Ctrl-V), **Delete** (Delete key), **Wear, Edit.**

> **Other Options*:** are by file type like **Teleport to Landmark, Attach To, Attach to HUD**.

1. **ALL ITEMS:** These are your SL assigned inventory folders and their file assignments. Some of the SL files are automatically assigned to receive certain items that you take, save, or upload.

> 🗀 **My Inventory:** Your list of folders and files

>> 🗀 **Animations: File: Upload Animation (L$10)** function saves the file in this folder.

>> 🗀 **Body Parts: Inventory: Create: New Body Parts** saves to this folder.

>> 🗀 **Calling Cards:** When you establish friendship, your friend's **Profile** is stored here.

>> 🗀 **Clothing: Inventory: Create Clothes** or *right-click* your Avatar. (**Appearance: Save**).

Inventory Tabs (Cont.)

- 📁 **Gestures: Inventory: Create Gesture** resides here.

- 📁 **Landmarks: World: Create Landmark Here** or when you re ceive a landmark.

- 📁 **Lost and Found:** Lose or leave an object, it is *right click* **Re turn** or **Auto-Return** to this folder.

- 📁 **Notecards: Inventory: Create: New Note** or when you receive and **Save** a **Note,** they are here.

- 📁 **Objects:** Any item you *right-click* **Buy**, **Copy**, or **Take** ends up here.

- 📁 **Photo Album: Snapshots: Upload (L$10)** your SL snapshots are saved here when you upload.

- 📁 **Scripts: Inventory: Create: New Script** and it is saved here.

- 📁 **Sounds: File: Upload Sound (L$10)** is stored here.

- 📁 **Textures: File: Upload Image** (Ctrl-U) is automatically filed in this folder

- 📁 **Trash:** *Right-click* **Delete** goes to the trash**.**

📁 **Library:** Files owned by Linden Lab. Locked but can **Copy** or **Wear**.

2. RECENT ITEMS: References files you uploaded, moved, copied, or modified since your last SL sign on.

*Option Menus are listed for reference only and will be further explained if supported in an exercise.

SHORTCUT COMMANDS:

Inventory	Ctrl-I
File "options"	*Right-click* on File Name
Copy	Ctrl-C
Paste	Ctrl-V
Delete	(delete key)
Upload Image (L$10)	Ctrl-U
Close Window	Ctrl-W
Build	B (with Chat window closed)

Clutter Can Become a Problem

Your **Inventory** folders are organized at this point. However, the more time you spend in-world, the more things you collect. Everyone has the urge to take everything that is offered to them. Before you know it, your **Inventory** becomes cluttered.

Start now. Every time you collect items, place them into new folders or sub folders by categories you can recognize. Some of the Boxed items you open automatically file the contents into a titled file folder for you. Even though this is helpful, you end up with extraneous folder categories. *Drag* these folders either to one of the Linden Labeled folders or set up your own category for storage. Make sure objects and folders are titled with key search words for easy finding.

Use the **Search** function for fast retrieval. Get familiar with **Filters** and what they can do. A detailed explanation of the **Inventory** Commands and Tabs can be found above.

CHAPTER 7:
MAKING A MOVE
Edit Appeal

Figuring Things Out

It's not time to **Create** (building objects from scratch) just quite yet. Best way to understand the world around you is to figure out some of the Objects you have collected, move them around, understand what they do and how they were created. This provides the fastest insight into the **Build** Tool Box. Be patient, and you can jump ahead faster this way and bypass the frustration.

EXERCISE 7: EXPLORING "EDIT" AND OBJECTS

By now you know the term "item" is a generic term used in reference to the things you can file in your **Inventory (Objects, Scripts, Textures, Notes, Snapshots, etc.)**.The **Library** folder **Objects** is used here but you can also repeat this exercise on your inventory of free Objects you collected.

- ◆ Open the **Inventory** window (Ctrl-I); *double left-click* **Library** folder; *double left-click* **Objects** folder.

- ◆ *Left-click hold* on an item in the **Objects** folder and then *drag* and *drop* it to the floor. Do this a couple of times. Try to pick things that don't sound too big (e.g. Domino, Chat Parrot, etc.).

- ◆ Do not pick an object that states (Drop to the Ground). This object has a "**physical**" setting (recognizes gravity) which means it will fall through any platform or raised surface you are on.

- ◆ Once the item is "rezzed"("appears"), *right-click* and a pie menu will appear; *select* **Edit**

- ◆ If the **Edit** Tool's **General Tab** on the object is not filled in with information, *right-click* the Object a second time.

- ◆ You have it when the Name of the Object, Creator, and Owner appear.

- ◆ The **Build** pane **Edit** opens for the object. Once you understand how items are constructed, you can start building using the "**Create**" tool.

- ◆ There are five tabs (**General, Object, Features, Texture,** and **Content**). You should have the **General Tab** selected. The name of the object should be listed, as well as the name of the "Creator." You will also see your Avatar's name as the "Owner".

♦ Note where this tab notes "1 Object." Next to it lists the number of **Prims**. When Objects are **Linked,** they are presented as 1 Object. The number of Primitives defines the number of shapes that make up that Object.

♦ *Right-click, select* **Edit** on another Object from your **Inventory**. How many Objects and Primitives does it have?

♦ *Right-click* an object again and the Pie Menu appears. Explore the Pie Menu and see what you can do with that object or what it can do. Explore a couple of different objects. Lights can be turned on, torches can be attached to your hand, Hats can be worn, and Doors can swing open. A "Script" is placed by the "Creator" under the edit tab **Content** to define what it can do. If the object is Static, the Pie Menu presented offers the basic **Take, Take Copy, Sit Here**, etc. These menu options are also dictated by the "Permissions" provided by the Creator.

♦ *Right-click* **Edit** again. Notice cross arrows in Red, Green, and Blue Appear. This allows you to move the Object around. *Left-click: Hold* and *Drag* an arrow point. SLOWLY or otherwise the object can quickly move out of view. Try moving each colored arrow point. The object changes shape. Now you have the idea.

♦ Now *left-click, Hold* the Object and press the **Control** (Ctrl-) key. The colored arrows appear in a circle pattern. Using your *left-click* and *Hold* routine on your mouse you can **rotate** the object by "*dragging*" on the colored arrows.

SHORTCUT COMMANDS:

Move Object*	*Drag arrow*
Copy Object*	Shift, *drag arrow*
Rotate Object*	Ctrl, *drag curve*
Edit	Ctrl-3
Object Information	*Right-click, select* **Edit** (or *double left-click*)
File Information	*Right-click, select* **Properties**

Required to be in Edit Mode

Taking it One Tool and Tab at a Time

The five **Build** Tabs that appear when you open and then select **Edit** on the pie menu have a lot of information to offer—more than you actually need to know right now. We are exploring only the **Edit** tool's **General Tab** here, so Building will make more sense when we get to it.

Look around you, everything you see, vehicles, buildings, bridges, streets, signs, benches, basically every THING is an Object made out of Primitive Shapes (Prims). Just *right-click* and learn about it by selecting **Edit**.

If you don't own the item, then **Edit** will tell you about it, but it will not allow you to make any changes or even move it. In another chapter we will demonstrate how **Edit** is used as one of the five **Build** tools and how you can create things, set the permissions, add scripts, and let your own imagination soar.

MORE OBJECTS TIPS AND HINTS:

- Objects can be dragged to the ground or worn. Sometimes they come packaged in a box, and you have to **Open** the box first and **Copy** the Contents into your **Inventory** before you can use them.

- Once you **Copy** a box's content, **Delete** the object boxes, these empty boxes just congest your Inventory.

- Anything you **Delete** can be found in the **Trash** Folder. It will stay in the **Trash** until you *right-click* **Inventory: File: Empty Trash**.

- If your **Edit** pane appears small, click the **More** button to expand it and **Less** to minimize it.

- When you *Drag* an Object from your Inventory and you are done with it, *right-click* the object and *select* **Take** returns a Copy of the Object to the **Inventory**. **Take** will **Copy** the Object back to the same folder it came from. You now have a duplicate.

- If you don't want a duplicate of the Object, then the **Delete** key, while in **Edit** mode, should be used instead (**Edit** mode displays the cross arrows on the Object).

- If you don't have "**Copy**" permission on an Object, then "**Take**" places the Original Object back into Inventory. If you try and **Delete** this Object it will warn you first that you don't have **Copy** permissions and it is being permanently deleted. This is a helpful warning.

- An Object equals 1 Prim. If Objects are linked, then the Linked Group is listed as a single Object but the Prim count will reflect the sum total of the individual Parts.

- If an object is dynamic (i.e. it moves, talks, changes color, etc.), then it has a Script placed under its **Content Tab**. This Script may or may not be readily evident since **Linked** Objects reflect only the elements of the "Parent" Object. To find a Script may require you to **Unlink** the parts. You may not hold the **Permission** to do this.

MORE OBJECTS TIPS AND HINTS: (Cont.)

- If an object has a **Physical** setting, it will drop to the ground. In the Library folder there are objects with a notation (Drop to Ground). This means that if you are on a platform, or a raised surface, it will sink to the ground and may disappear from your view if you are not standing on the ground.

- You can also *double left-click* any object in **Inventory** (or *right-click* any Item in **Inventory** and *select* **Properties)** for a quick summary of the Creator, Owner, and **Permissions** (See the **General Tab** Information below).

- **Permissions** will remain in effect when the item is being used as part of another, or within another object. For example, if you use a **No Transfer** texture as part of a linked build, then the entire build is Non-transferable too. The same applies if any element of an object is **No Copy**.

- Check **Permissions** on anything you plan to use to make sure the **Permission** setting isn't going to limit you.

- **Modify** means the next owner can **Edit** the item, stretch it, open it, pull it apart, **Unlink** it and so on. An object referred to as **No Mod** is protected from tampering. A lot of content that you **Buy** from other residents will be **No Mod** to protect the creator.

INFORMATION: GENERAL TAB

The **General Tab** lists the Basic, Background, Physical, and Permission properties of the Object.

Name: Defines the Object, used in Searches for object retrieval.

Description: Helpful notes added to an Object (Optional).

Creator: The originator of the Object sets the original **Permissions** and restrictions.

Owner: Current owner of the Object.

PERMISSIONS

The **permissions** (or rights) are first set by the Creator and then by the Owner. The Creator may be the same person or a different person from the Owner. The **permissions** tell you the rights you have over that Object.

The **permissions** system defines how objects can be used as they are passed on from one owner to another. Each and every item (Textures, Photos, Notes, Scripts, Objects, Clothing, etc.) has a set of **Permissions** listed under their **Properties** (*right-click* the **Inventory** item and *select* **Properties**) or view them through the **Edit** panel (*right-click* the item and *select* **Edit**).

There are three main **permission** settings and a combination of them can be defined by you before you pass the item on to another Owner. However, if you are not the original Creator or Owner the settings themselves may already be restricted.

INFORMATION: GENERAL TAB (Cont.)

1. Copy Permissions: Allows copies to be made of the item.

2. Modify Permissions: You can make changes to the item. For example, change color and texture, change size, modify scripts, Unlink the parts, etc.

3. Transfer Permissions: If you have transfer rights you are able to give or sell the object to another Avatar.

Combination Permissions
If you have the copy and transfer rights you can make as many copies and give or sell the item as many times as you want.

Full Permissions
This means you have the rights to copy, modify, and transfer an object.

OTHER OPTIONS:

Share with Group
Members of the group you designate will be able to use this object, move it around, and so on. The object needs to be set to a group name for this to have an effect.

Allow Anyone to Move
Anyone can move the item around. They don't need to be the owner or part of a group.

Allow Anyone to Copy
The item basically becomes free for the public to copy. Only assign this permission when you want people to take copies without having to buy it.

Only as the owner of the object can you set the rights for the next owner (restricted only by the limitations imposed upon the object by the previous owner or creator).

Raring to Go?

After exploring Stores, Malls, and Warehouses for Free Stuff and looking at the cool Inventory you collected, you are probably itching to try your hand at building something. In fact, you probably noticed there are training classes offered in building.

You may notice other Avatars in the Sandbox who are making all sort of neat stuff. Bet you think it's easy? Actually it is, once you know the tricks. Yep, it's time to take out those building tools and try it out for yourself. If you are not in a Sandbox, go ahead and find one, it's time to build.

CHAPTER 8:
TOOLING AROUND
Every THING is an Object

Don't be a Prima Donna

Everything you see in-world is made up of primitive shapes. These basic building shapes are called **Prims** for short. These shapes are created using the tools supplied in the **Build** (B) Function. Various block forms are made available including the cube, cylinder, prism, sphere, torus, tube, and ring. These can then be twisted, hollowed, linked, and textured. In addition, physical and light properties can be applied. All the buildings, gadgets, furniture, animals, costumes, vehicles, and even fashion accessories are created by manipulating and joining these primitive shapes.

Each primitive shape is counted as a single Prim. **Link** (Ctrl-L) two primitive shapes together and you've created one object with 2 Prims. A car might be made up of 30 Prims; a skyscraper might have over 1,000 Prims. The number of Prims you are limited to use will depend on where you are building and the amount of land you or your group owns in that region. It may also be limited by the allowance the Land Owner gives you (for example, when renting). All land is limited by a Prim count (listed on the **Objects Tab** of the **About Land** window).

All Avatars, no matter the membership type, have full access to the **Build** tools. You can build on your own land, on land owned by a group that has you listed as a member, and in public sandboxes. It's never a good idea to just start building in any open space, if you don't have that land owner's permission.

You can build in a Sandbox as much as you want. Just make sure you take your build with you or before they "wipe" the Sandbox clean. In a Sandbox you can build to your heart's content. Just keep the builds stored in your **Inventory** (Ctrl-I) and bring them out as you want to work on them.

EXERCISE 8: BUILD AND CREATE OBJECTS

CREATING OBJECTS

♦ *Right-click* the ground and *select* **Create**. This will open a **Build** pane with the **Create** Tool already selected. Displayed at the top are all the basic shapes available to use. Alternatively, you can also *click* the blue **Build** button at the bottom of your screen (B) or use (Ctrl-4).

♦ The default shape is a CUBE, textured with plywood, and colored white.

◆ Your cursor appears as a small wand. In this mode every time you *left-click* in this mode, a new CUBE appears unless you *select* a different shape in this pane. Each CUBE or shape is a one Prim (primitive) Object.

◆ If you *left-click* on the floor, the new object is placed perfectly on that floor. If you *click* the top of another object, the new object will be placed touching the top surface of it. If you *click* in the air the new object will appear to sit in the air. The object placement is controlled by your click.

◆ Once a shape appears the **Create** pane changes to the **Edit** pane with your new "object" selected and ready for you to change or modify how it looks. The **Edit** mode is recognized by the three cross arrows that appear on the object (red, green, and blue).

◆ If you want to **Create** more than one Prim without going to the **Edit** pane each time, then *click* the **Keep Tool Selected** box in the **Create** pane. This will allow you to continue creating new shapes.

◆ Go ahead, **Create** a couple of shapes, place them on the ground, in the air, and on top of each other.

◆ **SELECTING OBJECTS**

◆ While you are in the **Edit** mode, *left-click* on any of your objects to select it. Then *left-click* another, and another. Repeat those steps now with the Shift key down each time you select. Notice the objects ALL stay selected and they will respond as a group.

◆ Now release the Shift key and release your mouse selections by clicking on an object outside of your selection.

◆ Let's try a different selection approach. While still in the **Edit** mode, *Left-click* and *drag* and see what happens. You can start where there is no object like on the ground or in the air. Notice a yellow selection box growing and you can "wipe" your objects into it. All of your objects that are captured into the yellow are automatically selected. This is called "*Drag Selecting*".

◆ To release *Drag Selecting*, just *left-click* something other than the objects already selected.

MOVING OBJECTS

◆ While in the **Edit** (Ctrl-3) Mode, *select* one object. Then *left-click, drag* on one of the cross arrows that appear on the object.

◆ Release and *left-click, select* a number of objects (by individually grouping or by *drag selecting*). Again *left-click, drag* on the cross arrows that appear on your objects. Now drag on the arrows that appear off to the side of your object. Notice that the entire group moves together.

◆ Now hold the Shift key and drag an arrow end. Remember from the last chapter, this makes a copy. In this case, it made a **Copy** of the entire selection set. Let go of the shift. Now release the Set by *clicking* on something or somewhere outside of the selection.

◆ Let's **Rotate** a Prim. *Select* one Object and press the Control key (Ctrl-), *drag* on the curve or directly on the object. This rotates the single object. It can also be repeated for a selected group of objects.

♦ With the single object selected, press both the Control and Shift keys (Ctrl-Shift) and a pattern of small boxes appear. *Drag* on one and then another of the colored boxes. Notice what happens. The object can be re-sized and re-shaped. The white boxes expand and contract the shape uniformly; the red, green, blue boxes control sizing only on that sector or axis.

♦ Release, and now *Left-click, select* (*left-select*) or *drag select* two objects that are touching and repeat the exercise with Ctrl-Shift. Notice how both objects respond together.

LINKING AND UNLINKING

♦ Time to **Link**. Select 2 or more objects that are close together. Once they are "grouped", look at the **General Tab** in the **Edit** pane, how many objects and how many Prims are listed?

♦ Now perform the **Link** function (Ctrl-L). What does the **General Tab** list as the count of Objects and the Count of Prims?

♦ Move the linked group around, click on something else, and then come back to it. This is what "linking" is all about.

♦ Now **Unlink** your objects (Ctrl-Shift-L). *Click* on an object outside of the selection and come back to your group. Move it around. Did it separate? Then it's no longer linked.

Don't forget to clean up. You can *drag select* and **delete** for fast clean up. If you leave your work in the Sandbox it will all **Auto-return** to your **Lost and Found** folder in **Inventory** and become clutter.

Understanding Linked Prims

As you Link Prims, the last Prim selected for the object will be recognized as the parent link. The name of the parent link will become the name of the whole linked object. This is the reason why **naming your Prim creations** as you build is important. When you place your object in Inventory, the linked Prims become one file and the parent link is the name of the file for the whole object. The center (or origin) of the parent Prim becomes the center of the whole object, even if the parent link is not the physical center of the object itself. Depending on the placement this can make movement of the object difficult or awkward.

When building vehicles, any script in the vehicle will look to the parent link's orientation as the reference for determining the "front" of the vehicle. As a result, it can be important which Prim you select as the parent link.

BUILD AND CREATE TIPS AND HINTS:

- When you **Build** (Ctrl-4), you must be on buildable ground. Your top menu bar will display a little picture red circle crossing though a yellow cube if it is NOT allowed. If this icon is NOT displayed, it is land that allows you to build. Sandboxes allow building.

- When you *left-click* the **Build** button, it opens with the **Create** tool and the CUBE shape selected.

- The default shape is the Cube, and all new Prims will be textured with a default plywood texture.

- It is always a good idea to make back up copies of builds while working on them. This way you can always recall an earlier version. Start a "Work-In-Progress" Folder in your **Inventory** (Ctrl-I).

- Clean out your **Objects** Folder and **Lost and Found** Folder often since that is where "**Take**" and "**Auto-return**" respectively places the Objects.

- Title your builds when you begin, this makes it easier for you to retrieve and organize them.

- Although Prims are solid to you as an Avatar normally, during building they are not solid, so Prims can be moved through objects, through each other, inside each other and even underground.

- *Drag selecting* can be a time saver, but it is less accurate and you may end up selecting objects you don't want. You may also accidentally select objects belonging to someone else, which may cause linking to inexplicably fail. Turn on the **Select Only My Objects** option in the Menu Bar to help avoid this problem.

- Drag selecting can be done several times in different places to keep adding sets of objects to the selection. So long as you hold the shift key down each time you do it, your previous selection will remain and be added to each time.

- If you are moving your Object around and it shoots out of view while in **Edit** mode, you can **Undo** (Ctrl-Z) or hit the delete key to eliminate it as long as you can still see its **Edit** pane.

- When you **Delete** an object in-world, it does not end up in your **Trash** file. It is deleted for good.

BUILD AND CREATE TIPS AND HINTS: (Cont.)

- When you **Take** or **Take a Copy** of your objects that are set as a "group selection" into your Inventory, then when you drag it out, the entire group of objects will reappear with the objects in the same positions relative to the others. However, upon rezzing, the objects are no longer grouped.

- When you are drag selecting the group is NOT permanently linking Objects.

- To **Link** use (Ctrl-L) and to **Unlink** use (Ctrl-Shift-L). Alternatively you can *left-click* **Tools** on the Menu Bar at the top of your screen and *select* **Link** or **Unlink** from the drop down menu. Most Objects consist of more then one Prim, so you will use these commands when you **Create**.

- When trying to link, if you get a message saying your objects are too far apart to link, this is because there is a link limit based on distance (measured from the Prim centers) and relative Prim size. This limitation will scale in that larger Prims have a greater link distance than smaller ones; conversely, the smaller that the Prims are, the closer they must be in order to be linked.

- After linking objects initially together, you can continue to add more Prims to it using the same technique. However, a linked object cannot exceed 30 meters in any dimension.

- Vehicles, or any physics-enabled object, cannot have more than 31 Prims. Note that any rider sitting on the vehicle will be considered a linked Prim on that vehicle, so the vehicle itself should remain under 30 Prims. (A vehicle can turn on its physics, and then have multiple riders sit on it)

- There is no nesting of linked groups. This means if you linked a third object to two objects already linked and then unlinked them it will not yield two groups. Instead it will yield three.

- To **Link** Prims you have to have the right permissions (reference the **General Tab**). You also can't **Link** or **Unlink** if the Object is "**Locked**" (reference the **Object Tab**).

BUILD AND CREATE TIPS AND HINTS: (Cont.)

- Once you think you have your work *Drag-Select*, **Linked**, or **Locked**, then *right-click* it, select **More**, *select* **Take Copy**. Don't immediately try a **Take**, as chances are you may overlooked selecting a small piece somewhere. Once **Take Copy** places it in your Inventory as a single object, take it aside and rez it to check that your saved object is actually your complete build with no missing pieces. Also, if it is **Linked** or **Locked**, try moving it around and even try deleting a part of it. This is a good way to test your build.

You can build in a Sandbox as much as you want. Just make sure you take your build with you or before they "wipe" the Sandbox. In a Sandbox you can build to your heart's content. Just keep those special builds stored in your **Inventory** and bring them out as you want to work on them.

SHORTCUT COMMANDS:

Create	Ctrl-4
Edit	Ctrl-3
Link*	Ctrl-L
Unlink*	Ctrl-Shift-L
Drag Selecting*	*Left-drag*
Individual Selecting (for Group)*	Shift, *Left-select*
Undo last step*	Ctrl-Z

Required to be in Edit Mode

INFORMATION: BUILD TOOLS AND TABS

The "**BUILD**" (**B**) Function Button accesses the five Build Tools and the five Reference Tabs:

TOOLS:

1. **FOCUS:** Allows you to move around an object to view it from different sides and angles. Use it to also view the world around you while you're standing still. (To use this mode, *left-click, hold* on an object and move from object to object)

> **Focus (Ctrl-1):** *drag* to change views
> > **Orbit (Ctrl-)**; **Pan (Ctrl-Shift)**

2. **MOVE:** Quick and easy way to move an object, lift it, and Rotate it, as long as you don't need precision.

> **Move (Ctrl-2):** *drag* to move object **Lift (Ctrl-)**; **Spin (Ctrl-Shift)**

3. **EDIT:** Make more precise changes to an object. When creating objects the precision becomes essential.

> **Edit (Ctrl-3):** *drag* arrow to move object
> > **Rotate (Ctrl-):** *drag* on curves;
> > **Stretch (Ctrl-Shift):** *drag* small boxes
> > **Copy (Shift):** *drag* arrow (a copy is left behind)
> > **Stretch (Ctrl-Shift):** *drag* a color box
> > **Select (Shift):** *left-click* each object
> > **Group (Shift):** *left-click* and *drag* yellow box to highlight objects
> **Link (Ctrl-L):** as 1 object; **Unlink (Ctrl-Shift-L)**

INFORMATION: BUILD TOOLS AND TABS (Cont.)

4. **CREATE:** To make a primitive shape. Choose a defined shape from the **Build** Box, or **Copy** a shape (with Permissions) by selecting it through the "**Edit**" and checking the **Copy Selection** box in the **Create** Tool, then *click* on the ground in-world to place it.

   Build (B) or *Left-click* **Build** Button opens to the **Create** Tool

   Create (Ctrl-4): *left-click* on a defined shape and *left-click* in-world to place it.

5. **LAND:** This tool is only activated when you own land or have the Permissions needed to change the Land's Terrain.

   Land (Ctrl-5): to open Tool

   General   Object   Features   Texture   Content

TABS: **(Ctrl-[ )** or **(Ctrl-])** to cycle through tabs if you don't see the Tabs, *click* the "**More**" button to maximize the pane ("**Less**" to minimize).

1. **GENERAL:** Provides **Basic** information (Name, Description) as well as **Background** information (Creator, Owner); **Physical** Properties (Objects, Prims); and **Permissions** (Copy, Modify, Transfer) for the Object.

2. **OBJECT:** This tab defines the parameters essential for advanced edits to a Prim. It addresses numerically the Object's **Position, Size, Rotation, Cuts, Twists, Tapers, and Shears**. It also allows for setting **Locked, Physical, Temporary,** and **Phantom** parameters.

3. **FEATURES:** Addresses two major settings: **Flexible** (allowing the object to Flex around the Z Axis) and **Light** (allowing the object to emit light). These functions are used in Advanced Building.

4. **TEXTURE:** Change the color or texture of an Object or select and change the texture on part of an object.

5. **CONTENT:** Add Objects, Notes, Photos, Gestures, Scripts, etc. that can be stored, referenced or used to direct the Object.

These Tabs are further explored, as needed, in the following Chapters. Too much detail at this juncture will only be confusing. Some of the commands and tabs in the **Build** Tool Box are used in **Advanced Builds**.

BASIC BUILDS TO TRY

CONSTRUCT A FLOATING BUILD PLATFORM
(Place above a crowded Sandbox)
Create a Cube using (Ctrl-4); **Flatten** it using (Ctrl-Shift, *drag* blue boxes together); **Stretch** it (Ctrl-Shift, *left-drag* the white corner boxes outward) until it reaches its farthest point. **Move** it up into the sky (*drag* blue arrow upward). To make the platform larger **Copy** (Shift-*drag an* arrow until the Prims separate; or try Ctrl-D); *Select* (Shift, *left-click, select*) each Prim; then **Link** (Ctrl-L) these multiple flat Prims together. The next Chapter explains precision alignment of Prims by using the **Object Tab** numbers.

BOX OF OBJECTS
Create (Ctrl-4) a Cube; *drag* a couple of Objects as files out of your **Inventory** (Ctrl-I) onto the Cube. Now you have a boxed set of Objects that can be "Opened".

TALKING OBJECT
Create a Shape of your choice (Ctrl-4); open the **Content Tab** and *click* **New Script**; Close **Edit** (*left-click* "X"). Now touch the Object and it will say "Touched". *Right-click* your object again, and select **Edit**. While in **Edit** *click* open the Script and Change the words "Touched" to whatever you want your object to say. Now close **Edit** and touch your object again.

After you finish building these objects; Name them on the **General Tab** pane of the **Edit** Tool. Then close the **Edit** tool; *right-click* the object and **Take** it into your **Inventory**. You can re-file it then to another folder if you want. Go ahead and set up an **Exercise** Folder in **Inventory** for keeping all of your Exercise Builds from this book.

This is Only the Beginning....

The **Build** Box of Tools and Tabs have more to offer than we will even cover in this book. Once you get the basics down and have a bit of practice under your belt, there will be no stopping you. Add imagination and ingenuity and you too will be building a better mousetrap. On to the next chapter now to build bigger, better, and more elaborate things.

CHAPTER 9: OBJECTIONS PLEASE
The Numbers have It

Yes, Math Can Be Fun!

Math can actually be fun and make sense when you **Create** by the numbers. With the help of the **Object Tab**, 10 plus 5 can actually equal a Perfect Prim alignment. Okay, you were anxious to build so you already jumped ahead and tried it out. You probably put in enough time building already to have experienced the frustration of trying to line up Prim corners. Maybe you got as far as trying to add a roof to four walls or place a top on top of an open box. Some of you even made more ambitious attempts trying to build stairs, construct a window, or align table legs. Why does it look so easy when someone else does it?

Building is easy once you realize that all it takes is applying simple math. Add a little bit of geometry, later combine it with a bit of physics, and WOW, all of a sudden you have an unbelievable creation. Before you even realize it you are great at math and actually loving it! Why couldn't school math have been this much fun?

EXERCISE 9: ON YOUR MARK, GET SET, GO....

CREATE YOUR WORK SPACE

- Find a Sandbox. Then claim your space by rezzing a large Build Platform (described in Chapter 8). We also recommend that you **Link** (Ctrl-L) and then **Lock** (found on the **Object Tab**) the platform so you don't accidentally destroy it.

- Use this Platform when building to place and align your Prims using **0.00 degrees** as your rotation reference (trust us right now). Then after your new creation is linked, it will be easier to rotate it and place it at the angle you need to "fit" onto your land, place into a room, or position it with another build. Your build platform can be placed in the Sky above any public Sandbox or rezzed onto the ground to insure a flat surface. Create a "Build" folder in your **Inventory** (Ctrl-I. Label and store your platform there along with other useful building tools.

TAKE THE TIME TO PREP

◆ Remember to set the **Select Only My Objects** setting in the drop down Menu Bar to avoid accidentally selecting another Avatar's box or build.

◆ Turn on the Noon lights in the drop down **World** Menu (Ctrl-Shift-Y) so that you can see what you are doing.

◆ Decide on a name to use in this **Build** Session. From the very first Prim you create on this build, name it and use one consistent title throughout the build. Then when you Shift-*drag* to copy from those first Prims, the whole build continues the name. Set up a separate folder for your "Work in Progress." You should save regularly and often into that folder when working on big projects.

PRACTICE PRECISION BUILDING

◆ **Create** a Cube (Ctrl-4), *click* on your platform floor.

◆ **Create** a Second Cube by clicking somewhere around your First Cube. It should not touch and can be in the air.

◆ Open **Edit**, **Object Tab** on the First Cube and notice the default Size is **.5000 meters** and the rotation default is **0.00 degrees**.

◆ Change the Size of the First Cube to **1.0 meter** for **X, Y,** and **Z** (*Size 1.000 XYZ*). *Left-click* the Second Cube and change it also to **Size 1.000 XYZ**. Notice the Cubes became larger.

◆ Write down the **X, Y,** and **Z** *Positions* listed on the **Object Tab** of the First Cube.

◆ *Left-click* the Second Cube. Change the **X** and **Z** *Positions* on the Second Cube to equal the First Cube's **XZ** *Positions*. **Z-Position** places the two Cubes at the same height. The **X-Position** places the Cubes on the same X-axis (path).

◆ Now change the **Y-Position** on the Second Cube by Subtracting **meter** from the **Y-Position** number you noted on the First Cube. Now the two sides of the Cube are precisely touching and the Cubes are precisely aligned.

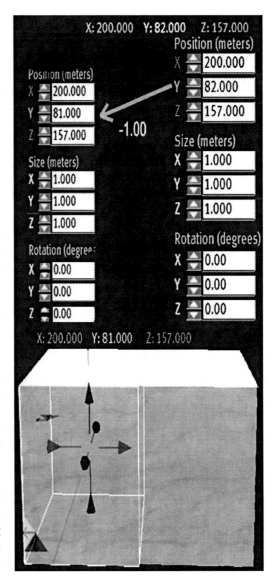

PRACTICE PRECISION BUILDING (Cont.)

◆ Now add **1.0 meter** to the Second Cube **Y-Position**. Both Cubes should have the same X,Y, and Z position numbers. Notice what is happening. This placed the two cubes perfectly together (one inside the other).

◆ Now try stacking the Cubes (Hint: Change the **Z-Position**)

How about that for EASY? Go ahead, play around with the position numbers. Notice also that the largest you can stretch any Shape is *Size 10.0 XYZ*. Experiment by creating some different shapes and aligning them together.

The Numbers ALMOST Have It

The above exercise was easy because the cubes you matched had the same dimensions (*Size .500 XYZ, 1.0 XYZ or 10.0 XYZ*). But we don't live in a perfect world. Dimensions will vary across the board. Objects also come in different shapes and sizes. We probably caught you off guard in the above exercise when you tried our suggestion and started experimenting with aligning different shapes. What happened? They didn't align perfectly. That's because the positions measure from the Object Center Point. If the Objects are the same dimensions, you don't realize it.

See the table below for what you need to do to achieve perfect alignment using **EXERCISE 9: PRACTICE PRECISION BUILDING** for reference. Remember that you are aligning by the Center Points of these Objects. Therefore this represents the respective *Size* divided by 2 ("in half"), then added together. Once you have that SUM, you need to add or subtract it from the stationary Object's position number (depending on which side of the stationary object you want to align the movable object against).

CHALLENGE:
Perfectly align a side of **OBJECT 1** to a side of **OBJECT 2** (for the X, Y, then Z Positions)

OBJECT 1: (stationary)	OBJECT 2: (movable)	POSITION NUMBERS for OBJECT 2
Size: X_1 = 1.000 meters Y_1 = 1.000 meters Z_1 = 1.000 meters	*Size:* X_2 = 1.500 meters Y_2 = 1.000 meters Z_2 = 0.500 meters	*Formula:* $X_2\text{-Position} = X_1\text{-Position} + (\frac{1}{2}X_1 + \frac{1}{2}X_2)$ $Y_2\text{-Position} = Y_1\text{-Position} + (\frac{1}{2}Y_1 + \frac{1}{2}Y_2)$ $Z_2\text{-Position} = Z_1\text{-Position} + (\frac{1}{2}Z_1 + \frac{1}{2}Z_2)$
X_1-Position: 200.00 *Y_1-Position:* 82.00 *Z_1-Position:* 157.00	(.500 + .750) = 1.250 (.500 + .500) = 1.000 (.500 + .250) = 0.750	*X_2-Position:* 201.25 *Y_2-Position:* 83.00 *Z_2-Position:* 157.75

Go ahead and give it a try. Change the sizes on your two cubes in **EXERCISE 9** and give it a go. Of course you probably have to use your own **Position** numbers since we don't know where in the world you're building.

There, you now had a refresher in Algebra 101. Come on, it wasn't THAT bad! Now are you ready for Geometry and Physics? Just kidding, we have other things you need to know and work on first. Before you celebrate, review some of the Hints, Commands, and the **Object Tab** Information below. Then you deserve a break…and celebrate your accomplishment.

BUILD WITH NUMBERS TIPS AND HINTS:

- All shapes have a Center point. If your Cube is *Size 1.0 XYZ*, the Center point is **.5 XYZ**. This becomes important to know when you align two different sizes or shapes.

- Where you *left-click* to **Create** a Prim will affect how it is aligned. A *Left-click* on the floor will ground the new Prim on the floor. *Left-click* on top of another Prim and it will be grounded on that existing Prim. *Left-click* on vertical wall will align your new Prim snugly against that wall. *Left-click* on the face of another Prim, will fit the new Prim to that face.

- There is a limit on the scale of an object. Prims cannot go below 0.01m in *Size* on any axis, so if any part of your object reaches that *Size* you will not be able to shrink it further. Similarly, Prims cannot exceed 10m on any axis.

- Change the **Position**, **Size**, and **Rotation** of an Object by *dragging* it about with your mouse (while in Edit) or type numbers directly into these fields for more precision.

- When you have a section of your build completed, **Lock** it to ensure it is safe from accidental changes.

- The large majority of objects and Prims in-world defy the rules of physics and ignore gravity. If you *drag* a Prim into the air, it stays there. This is because by default Prims are not **Physical**.

- Vehicles are often **Physical** because they need to react to terrain and obstacles. Be careful when setting items as **physical**. **Physical** objects cause extra load on the server if they get stuck, or are very active in colliding with other objects. In addition, **Physical** objects can roll, bounce or be pushed and end up on your neighbor's land.

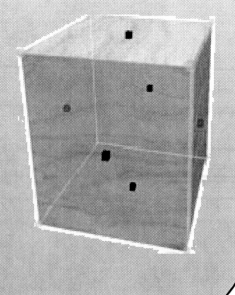

- **Phantom** objects (meaning that you can walk through) show up listed as **Phantom** in the box that appears when you *hover* your mouse over them.

BUILD WITH NUMBERS TIPS AND HINTS: (Cont)

- An object has different states: "normal", **locked**, **physical, temporary, phantom**, and combinations of these (except when **Flexible** under the **Feature Tab** is checked, which limits the object state).

- The **Object Tab** options can have a negative or positive value. Where you have **Cut**, **Hollow** or made any other change that causes additional surfaces to exist on the object, you will be able to **Texture** those new surfaces (Discussed further in the next chapter).

- Some options such as **Cut** and **Hollow** are widely available on all shapes, whereas others such as **Dimple** are only applicable to spherical ones.

INFORMATION: OBJECT TAB

NUMERIC FIELDS

Position: Measured in meters against the World coordinates according to the region you are in,

Size: Measured in meters (minimum of .01m and maximum of 10m)

Rotation: Measured in degrees. Initial placement at 0.00 degrees

AXIS: refers to the SL coordinate system. Objects can be moved along different axes while in **Edit** mode. The three basic axes referenced in the **Object Tab** are:

> **x-axis (back/forward, horizontal)**
> **y-axis (left/right, horizontal)**
> **z-axis (up/down, vertical)**

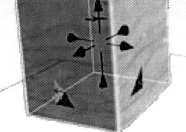

INFORMATION: OBJECT TAB (Cont.)

BUILD FUNCTIONS

Locked
Lock one or more objects and those objects cannot be edited, moved or changed in any way.

Physics
Makes the Object react to physics, so that it is affected by gravity, can bounce and be pushed, and will react to Avatars or other objects colliding with it.

Temporary
When an object is marked as temporary, it is not permanent and it will be deleted a few minutes after use (i.e. used in ammunition, beach balls, particles, or anything that might get away from you).

Phantom
This setting determines whether the object is considered solid or can be walked through. (used for doors or walls that you want to make invisible or have residents walk through).

Material
The Material influences how an object acts and what it sounds like when bumped, touched, jumped on, etc. (for example: a rubber ball will respond differently then a stone; Light emits a halo effect).

Building Block Type
Allows you to swap out one shape in your build for another shape while retaining size, texture, and other settings on that Prim.

The remaining **Advanced Edit** controls on the **Object Tab** will change depending on the type of base shape you are using. These are commonly used in more Advanced Builds.

Cut (begin/end)
Takes a slice out of the object along the Z axis. Specify where the cut starts and finishes.

Hollow
Hollows out the object starting from the center of the shape and expanding out. Specify what percentage of the radius is hollow.

INFORMATION: OBJECT TAB (Cont.)

Twist (begin/end)
Puts twists into the object and warps its shape as well as texture alignment.

Taper
Reduces the top or bottom sides (X or Y axes, negative or positive) size of the Prim.

Top Shear
Shifts (shears/skews) the top surface of the object away from the bottom. The X and Y axes can be shifted separately.

Dimple (begin/end)
Cuts a hole in a sphere from ring of latitude (specify the percentage) to the top or bottom of the Z axis. The dimple cuts straight to the origin of the object (leaving a cone-shaped hole).

Build Prim Efficiently

It's time for you to become aware of the importance of building with Prim efficiency in mind because you are limited by the number of Prims you can place on a parcel of land. A common SL term is "Primfficiency", which is defined as mastering the art (and science) of Prim shaping to minimize Prim count.

Think of it as opting to put up four separate Prims to construct a 10m x 10m room, and then use two more Prims by putting in a floor and ceiling. The Primfficiency option is to **Hollow** out a *Size 10.0 XYZ* Cube. It's a 6 Prim versus 1 Prim decision. When you build with primfficiency you start looking at your builds differently.

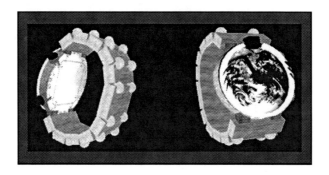

PRIMFFICIENCY BUILDS TO TRY

STAIRS: Two stair steps can be made with a single Prim.

Create a Cube (Ctrl-4) and set the **Object Tab** pane **Path Cut Begin = 0.125** and **Path Cut End = 0.875**; **Rotate** (Ctrl-*drag* on the Prim) to bring it around so you can see the two steps; then stretch it (Ctrl-Shift *drag* colored boxes) to widen the steps; This may not look impressive now, but when you are ready to make stairs, a stack of 20 stairs will only have 10 Prims now.

Name the stairs in the **General Tab** pane; then save them by closing the **Build** Box (*left-click* "**X**") and *right-click* the stairs and *select* **Take** from the pie menu that appears.

BARSTOOL: As a one Prim seat.

Create (Ctrl-4) and *select* a Tube. Stretch it so it's taller. Set **Hole Size Y = 0.50**. **Profile Cut Begin = 0.25** and **Profile Cut End = 0.95**. Then carve out your new seat by making **Hollow = 85**.

Now add a *left-click* Action. In **Edit** *select* the **General Tab** (or *right-click* and **Edit** the stool). Near the bottom, under where it says "**When Left-Clicked**" *select* "**Sit On Object.**" Now close the **Edit** pane and *left-click* your barstool for a seat. Yes, it's that easy.

WHEEL: Make a more realistic wheel.

Create a Ring; Set **Twist Begin = 90 and Twist End = 90** and **Hole Size X = 0.75**. For a better effect now **Lower Profile Cut End = 70** and make **Hollow = 25.** You can size these to your preference. It can also be built into a plate, a vase, a hat, a necklace, a ring, or whatever you want it to be.

After you finish building these objects; Name them in the **General Tab** pane of the **Edit** Tool. Then close the **Edit** tool; *right-click* the object and **Take** it into your **Inventory.** You can re-file it then to another folder if you want.

Plan Ahead When Building

Good planning can always save you time and pain later on. How large is the space you have available for the build, and how many Prims can you sensibly afford to use on building your house or store and still leave enough for furnishings or product? When you are ready to buy or rent land, set up a store or a house, these are questions you need to address.

In order that resources within each Region are shared fairly among the land owners the number of Prims available is proportional to the amount of land owned in a given Region. This means that the only way to increase the number of Prims you will have available to you, is to rent or purchase more land in the same Region. For example, if you own two parcels on opposite sides of the region, you can use the entire Prim count for both parcels added together in a build that sits on just one of them. For that reason you will often see water or parks being purchased by local Residents to bump up the number of Prims they can use in their builds.

Let's do some simple math to determine the amount of Prims a property can support.

Prims per Region: 15,000 Prims
Region Size: Approximately 65,500 sq. meters of land
Calculate Parcel Size: Width x Length in meters

CHALLENGE: Amount of Prims allowed on a Parcel of Land

FORMULA: [(15,000/65,500) x (Parcel Size 1 + Parcel Size 2)];
or (.229 x Parcel Size)

4096 sq. meters =	**.229 x 4096 sq. meters = 937 Prims**
2048 sq. meters =	**.229 x 2048 sq. meters = 468 Prims**
1024 sq. meters =	**.229 x 1024 sq. meters = 234 Prims**
512 sq. meters =	**.229 x 512 sq. meters = 117 Prims**
100 sq. meters =	**.229 x 100 sq. meters = 22 Prims**

So if you want to build a skyscraper that is 1,000 Prims, then even a 4096 sq. meter parcel will not be enough to support it. However, don't give up just yet. In the next chapter we discuss Textures. What you will find is more ways to primfficiency by using textures to replace some of the Prims you might have needed for your skyscraper build. In fact, you might even bring your Prim count to even half that amount by applying the right look and feel with Textures.

Other Considerations

Don't forget to also look at the lot size as you plan your build. What size are you planning for the X and Y dimensions of your build? Parcels of land are often rectangular in shape, which for a 1024 sq. meter parcel may mean 16m x 64m on the ground. If your build is 20m x 64m (or if you buy a build 20m x 64m) you won't fit it on your land even if you do have enough Prims. So consider where the build is to be placed, or shop for land that will accommodate it. Bottom line: plan accordingly.

Take a note of how many Prims belonging to you are already on the land you wish to build on. Plan how much you will budget for furnishings. This helps later when you *select* the build in order to **Copy** to your **Inventory**, you will be able to check it against the parcel (**World: About Land** object count again and know whether you have in fact selected all the parts to the build or not. If the number of Prims on the property minus the number you started with equals the number of Prims you have selected in the build then you've got it all.

Most large scale builds have sections that are patterned and repeated throughout the build. This gives a big build a more cohesive look, and of course saves you time because you can build one part ahead of time then just copy and stack. You can even pre-make pieces like towers, windows, and balconies that you **link** to make them easier to manipulate into a design. Sometimes it's even easier to buy certain elements and add them to your build (like staircases, revolving doors, detailed lights, etc.).

Some builders specialize in one type of build in order to perfect the product. The build might be a complete building or a build component (for example: castles, water fountains, garage doors, pianos, office furniture, computers, etc.). Often these items make more sense to buy instead of spending your time trying to duplicate the look. Then you can concentrate on the builds or components that interest you the most.

Also don't forget to check your **permissions**. Before you start, check that the textures, scripts, building components, etc. that you bought and intend to use in another build. Make sure that you have the **permissions** you need. You don't want to end up with a huge build that you can't **transfer** (or sell) because the door or a single texture (next Chapter's subject) is a **No Transfer** item.

CHAPTER 10:
TEXTURES HAVE REAL APPEAL
Build Live, Built Right, Build Second Life

Make it Look Good

In Second Life building is easy to learn and you can **create** anything you can imagine. You learned quickly in Chapter 9 that Second Life provides a powerful, highly flexible set of building tools that use pretty straightforward geometric primitives. Nothing to download, no special software applications to buy or learn, all you have to do is apply those creative juices. Build live, build in real-time, build right in Second Life.

When you build something, you can easily begin selling it to other residents, because you own the IP Rights of your creations. You also control what the next owner can or cannot do with your product. And if you want something, but don't quite have the time or skills to make it in Second life, you can then just do a quick **Search** (Ctrl-F) to find and **buy** what you need.

Textures are important to making a Prim look like an Object and the Object look like a Good Build. In fact, your build can even look professional, it's all in the choice and application of the texture.

EXERCISE 10: BUILD PROFESSIONALLY

For this exercise dig around in your **Inventory** (Ctrl-I) and find some textures to work with. You should have collected some window, fence, water, and glass textures when you shopped for Freebies in Chapter 5. If you find you don't have a lot of textures to work with, then **Search** (Ctrl-F) "Free Textures" again and try to find some.

TEXTURING ALL FACES

- ◆ **Create** a Cube (Ctrl-4)

- ◆ On the **Edit** pane, *left-click* the **Texture Tab**.

- ◆ *Left-click on* the **Color Window** that shows up white. Use the **Color Picker** (color pop-up window) to change the color. Go ahead and try a couple of different colors. See how it affects your Cube? *Select* White again.

- ◆ Now *Left-click on* the **Texture Picker** that shows the Plywood default. Use the (texture pop-up window) to change the texture by selecting a texture from the **Inventory** window that opens to all of your Texture files. Go ahead and try out a couple of textures on your Cube. Notice what happens.

♦ All of the faces on your Cube changed to the new color or texture setting when you changed your selection.

TEXTURING SELECTED FACES

♦ In **Edit** pane (Ctrl-3); *left-click* and *tick* the "**Select Texture**" button for the same Cube.

♦ This time *left-click* on only one face of your Cube. A target style overlay will appear to show it is selected.

♦ If you wish to select more faces, hold the Shift key down while you *left-click* and *select* one or more faces. The selected faces will all show a target overlay.

♦ Using the **View** feature will not deselect them and you can view your Cube from different angles. (Alt, *left-click hold and* move your cursor around to better see the box from different angles or closer.

♦ Now *select* a texture from your **Inventory** through the **Texture Picker**. Notice that only the selected faces will change to reflect the new settings.

♦ Now *left-click, select* only one face of your Cube at a time and change each of the six faces so that no two faces are the same. You can change the color or the texture.

DRAG-DROP TEXTURES

In addition to the above methods, textures can be *drag-dropped* from your **Inventory** (Ctrl-I) onto objects directly to texture them. Holding down the Shift key while doing this will change all faces of the object, otherwise, only the face that you drop the texture onto will be changed.

♦ **Create** another Cube (Ctrl-4);

♦ Open **Inventory** (Ctrl-I): **Texture** Folder

♦ Shift, *Drag-Drop* a File from the Texture folder onto the Cube

♦ Now (without the Shift) *Drag-Drop* a different Texture File onto one face of the Cube. See the difference?

TRANSPARENCY SETTINGS

♦ **Create** a Cube (Ctrl-4); *Set* **Object Tab** *Size 1.000 XZ* and *Size .0100 Y*

♦ In the **Texture Tab** *left-click* the **Texture Picker** and *select* the "**Blank**" Button. Notice it is now a Flat White Cube.

♦ Now in the **Texture Tab** *set* the Cube to a **50% Transparency**.

♦ View it up close using Alt *left-hold* and move into it with your mouse. It looks like a window and you can see through it!

TRANSPARENCY TEXTURES

♦ **Create** another similar Cube (Ctrl-4); *Set* **Object Tab** *Size 1.000 XZ* and *Size .010 Y*

♦ In the **Texture Tab** *left-click* the **Texture Picker** and *select* one of the Free Window Texture files from your **Inventory** that you collected in your travels.

♦ Voila! You created your first textured window. Looks good doesn't it. Go ahead and try some more textures that have transparencies in them. Try another Window, a Fence, Glass or Water. You can find Water Textures and Water Particles in your **Library** folder.

TEXTURING TIPS AND HINTS:

• A texture is an image used to change the look to the faces of Prims. They can have various material looks. When the application matches the product they can make objects appear more "real." A texture can also be used to make skin, hair, clothing, or be put in a Notecard.

• The **Texture Tab** in the **Edit** pane allows you to set the color and transparency. Good texturing can make the difference between average content and great content. You will find a default set of textures provided for you in the **Library** folder of your **Inventory**.

• When texturing an object, you can apply a texture to all of the faces it has (cube has 6 sides) or you can isolate a *set* a texture for one or more specific faces.

• Large builds need a lot of Prims. You keep your Prim count down by using high quality detail and shadowing on the textures along with some well placed alpha transparencies. For example, a framed window texture can be as "real" as a constructed Prim window. Combining primfficiency, good texturing, and well placed Prim usage, you can achieve that highly sought-after professional look to your build.

• When Objects share the same Center Point you can easily confuse the Objects when you select for **Edit**. Select the Prim for Editing by *Left-Clicking* on some other place than the Center Point of the Prim. Naming the Prim parts by different names will also help keep them clearly defined. Once they are appropriately named, then just check the **General Tab** to confirm your Prim selection.

• When you upload Images they should be as small as possible. It makes the **Upload** (Ctrl-U) go faster. SL will also adjust the width and height sizing to the nearest power of two.

TEXTURING TIPS AND HINTS: (Cont.)

- You can save Second Life images to your hard drive for editing, viewing, printing, etc. in your favorite imaging program. Just open the texture in your **Inventory** (*right-click* "**Open**"); Open the **File** menu and *Select* "**Save Texture As**" and type in any file name. This works only if you have **Modify Permissions** on the texture.

- When using a Texture that has a transparent effect, it may look better if you apply that texture to only the front and back faces. The rest of the Prim should have a completely transparent texture applied. Transparent textures can usually be found "Free" around SL. Also look for **Absolute White** and **Absolute Black** textures to add to your collection.

- In an attempt to keep your **Free Collection of Textures** organized, Set up a second **Textures** Folder. Then when you **Upload** Textures or Open a Box of Textures into the SL **Textures** Folder, it's easier to sort through and re-file.

- When you **Open** a box of Textures and **Copy to Inventory,** the picture windows that open in the process can be overwhelming on your screen. You have to close them individually.

- If you have a texture in Inventory that you want to copy to your hard drive to work with in a graphics program, you can. *Double-click* and open the window on that file from your **Inventory** Folder; then select **File** from the Menu Bar at the top of your screen; *select* **Save Texture As....** and it will save to your hard drive.

INFORMATION: TEXTURE TAB

Note: A texture is uploaded to Second Life through **File** (on the **Menu Bar**), *Left-click* **Upload Image** (L$10) or use the **Alternate Key Command** (Ctrl-U). The **Upload** can be found in your **Textures** folder.

THE TEXTURE AND COLOR PICKER

When changing texture or color, the respective **Picker** window opens. You can enter search words to find textures quickly, or navigate through using the file "tree." As you *select* a texture, a preview window opens to show the selection along with the textures dimensions in pixels. For Colors, the **Picker** window displays the various basic color choices which can also be expanded.

Blank Button: Eliminates the texture from the Prim, it looks like a blank opaque covering.

Default Button: Applies the plywood texture you get when you create a new Prim.

Apply Immediately: This selection sets a "live" mode which means as you *left-click* and preview a texture the application is immediately applied to the Prim.

Select Button: An extra step to apply a texture that you are previewing in the texture picker window. Use this approach when you are not sure of the texture you want to apply or you want to see the textures before you choose them. Then you don't lose your original texture.

Eyedropper Button: Option to *select* a texture that is on one Prim face and apply it to another. *Tick* **Apply Immediately** and *Click* on the **eyedropper** icon button and your cursor will change. You can now *click* on the face of any object while in the **Texture** or **Color Picker View** (that you "own" meaning it is in your **Inventory**). It will apply that texture or color to your object. This eliminates scrolling through the list trying to find a texture or color shade to "match."

OTHER TEXTURE OPTIONS

Transparency
The higher the value you indicate, the more see-through the object or selected faces become. You cannot go above 90% transparency with this method. If you want something to be totally transparent, you will need to find and use a transparent texture.

INFORMATION: TEXTURE TAB (Cont.)

Full Bright

Tick this feature to cause one or more of the surfaces to "light" up. This causes the Prim face to stand out when it's dark. It also eliminates the affect of shadows created from external light. This feature is particularly useful when making noticeable signs and billboards.

Mapping

This default causes the textures to react to changes in the dimensions such as the top's size being lowered, whereas **Planar** will pin the texture to the plane, so that you don't get a distorted texture when you twist, or shear the Prim shape.

> **Default** mode allows texture repeats to be set such that a setting of 1.0 stretches the texture to one repeat regardless of the size of the face.

> **Planar** mode applies the same texture but according to the "per meter" of the Prim. For example, a 2m cube will automatically have 2 repeats of the texture.

Shininess

To create Shiny Objects choose this preference option. Making objects shiny allows them to reflect light producing an attractive looking sheen in the object. The higher the setting, the glossier they will become.

Bumpiness

To add bumpy qualities to a surface choose from a number of **Bump-Mapped** styles that are listed.

Rotation

As you'd expect, this allows one or more face textures to be rotated in their alignment so you can "fit" it to your object.

Texture Repeats

How many times the texture patterns across the surface, either per meter (**planar**) or per face (**default**) depending on the Map setting selected.

Texture Offsets

This controls the exact positioning of the textures being overlaid for "fine" tuning the application.

Building Is Easy When You Know What To Do

You've got an understanding of Building and the basic application of textures. You're probably starting to develop some of your own creative ideas for builds. Maybe you even want to duplicate a real world object by seeing if you can make it in Second Life. At this point, you might even be thinking about duplicating your own house. First try the more advanced primfficiency builds in the next box to give you even more ideas to think about. Then look in your Inventory folder and pull out and try some of the Textures you find there. Pull out some of your objects from Inventory and study them. How are the textures applied?

PRIM EFFICIENT TEXTURING TO TRY

FRAMED PICTURE

Create two Cubes (Ctrl-4); and NAME them "Frame" and "Picture". Using the table below, change these two Cubes (Objects) to the size, settings, and textures as noted.

	OBJECT 1 (Frame)	OBJECT 2 (Picture)
STEP 1: OBJECT TAB	*Size:* $X_1 = 1.000$ $Y_1 = 1.000$ $Z_1 = 0.100$ Hollow = 80 **Rotation: Y = 90 Degrees** (lift Object into the Air) *Positions:* *Note X_1, Y_1, Z_1 Positions*	*Size:* $X_2 = 1.000$ $Y_2 = 0.010$ $Z_2 = 1.000$ **Rotation: Y= 90 Degrees** *Positions:* Same as X_1 and Z_1 Y_2 = Y_1 <u>Position</u> minus Y_2 <u>Size</u>
STEP 2: TEXTURE TAB	**Color Picker: Brown** *Tick* **Full Bright**	**Color Picker: Brown** *Tick* **Full Bright** *Tick* **Edit** Pane "**Select Texture**" *Select* ONE Face *Select* White Color *Select* a Snapshot Texture (from **Inventory: Library: Snapshots**)

Now turn off the lights (**World: Force Sun: Midnight**). Your framed picture should look like it's lit up. Then turn the World lights back on (Ctrl-Shift-Y) for the next Build.

PRIMFFICIENT WINDOW

Using the Framed Picture Build, Open into the **Edit** Mode for Object 2 (Picture). Make sure you have Picture selected since the Center Points of the two Objects are the same. You will see "**Multiple**" written across the **Texture Picker** window in the **Texture Tab** or check the Name of the Object under the **General Tab**. Now *Select* **White Texture** and **Grey Color**; *Set* the **Transparency to 50**. You now have a 2 Prim Window. That EASY!

Go ahead and *right-click* **Edit** and *Left-click drag* and *select* both the frame and window. **Link** the two pieces (Ctrl-L); Rename this object to a **Framed Window** using the **General Tab** pane, check to make sure you have captured **1 Object and 2 Prims**. Then close the **Build** Box and *right-click* "**Take**" your **Framed Window** into **Inventory** for a later exercise.

Now it's Making a Lot More Sense

Look around you at all the builds in Second Life. These builds are probably making a lot more sense to you now, and you are looking differently at the objects around you. Go ahead and experiment and try and duplicate some of the effects. Explore a combination of the **Object Tab** and **Texture Tab** to see what you can come up with. The whole idea is to have fun. Now you understand what Sandboxes are all about. Stay there a little while longer—maybe up on your private platform in the sky that you built in a previous Chapter.

Want more privacy? Go ahead and put walls on your platform (try it by the numbers). In the next chapter we are going to finally take a serious look at your Appearance and get you to experiment now with your clothes, hair, body style, etc. Depending on how self-conscious you are, you may not want to change in the middle of a public area. A private walled platform in the sky may be just the right answer.

CHAPTER 11:
JUST LOOK AT ME NOW
You Are What You Wear

FINALLY, you have some of the basics down, now let's work on you. Everyone looks like a Newbie at first. Some more so then others when they play with their appearance before they really understand what they are doing. So what that you ran into ten other people that looked exactly like you. Remember they don't know you, and you will keep creating and re-creating your look in an effort to perfect your style.

The difference now is that you are further ahead in Second Life because you took the time to go through all of those chapters on the basics. Now, "Newbie," it time to prepare for your Entrance. Let's see who you really are.

Your Style Your Way

You are born with **Clothing**, **Body Parts** and depending on your initial Avatar selection, you may have already some **Attachments** (see Chapter 12). These template, or default Avatars, can be found in your **Inventory** under **Library: Clothing** Folder. Looking through the files, notice Clothing actually covers a bit more territory than just clothes. There's skin and hair there too. Subtleties, you might say. Let's take a look.

REPLACE DEFAULT AVATAR SELECTION

If you want to change your default selection on your Avatar, the sex of your Avatar, or you just plain want to start over (after messing up). You can easily reapply a default Avatar template.

- *Left-click* **Inventory** (Ctrl-I); If you have too many folders opened then it's easier to *click* on the **Inventory File** menu, and *click* "**Close All Folders**"

- Now *left-click* **Library** folder

- *Left-click* **Clothing**

- Read the folder headings and decide on one or more

REPLACE DEFAULT AVATAR SELECTION
(Cont.)

- *Left-click* a folder and *Shift-* (⬇); *select* all the files in that folder

- *Right-click* **Copy**

- Now **Create** "**New Folder**" in your **Inventory** and *right-click* **Paste** those files into it

- Don't forget to **Rename** the **New Folder** and find a SL Folder like "**Clothing**" to drag it into

Try and keep your **Inventory** organized from the start. It will make it a lot easier to find things. Now when you want, you can *right-click* that **New Folder Name** and select "**Replace Outfit**." You have just done a total makeover. Everything you are wearing is replaced by everything in that file folder.

Don't be a Minimalist

Now you have the idea. All of your clothing and body parts exist in your inventory and are applied to your Avatar. They can be put on and taken off, but remain in your inventory either way. There's a couple of catches, though. Avatars do have a minimum requirement. So if you *click* that same folder and *select* "**Take Off Items**" you WILL actually be standing there stark naked. The minimum requirement does not involve clothes. Try not to do this in public, especially in a PG area. You can try the complete dismantling in your private walled platform. Then you can officially call your platform a "Sky-Box." This term is used to define a private zone.

Avatar minimums are what an Avatar cannot do without. An Avatar must have one shape, one skin, one set of hair and one set of eyes at all times (PG Avatars are on the teen grid and they have underwear as part of their minimum). The system won't let you remove them. You can adjust them, and you can also replace them by putting another one on. For example, you can still be bald, what you do is set the hair length and volume to zero. Now it appears that you have no hair, but in actuality you're still wearing a set. It's like shaving it all off. You can also attach a bald cap. So there are ways around the system to achieve the look you want.

Layer it On

You also have clothing layers. Each piece of clothing is designed to fit into a specific layer, and only one piece of clothing can occupy that layer at a given time. The clothing layers also follow the "real" order and placement of clothes. They are: Underpants, Undershirt, Socks, Pants, Skirt, Shirt, Jacket, Shoes, and Gloves. Select "Wear" for a new item and it replaces the item already on in that layer. You can only wear one pair of pants (and one skirt) at a time, one pair of socks, one shirt, one jacket, and so on.

Whenever you add or remove clothing, or change an item, there will be a short delay before the change is seen by everyone else.

EXERCISE 11: CHANGING YOUR APPEARANCE

Inventory items to wear can be found in your **Library** folder. You should have also found "Free" clothes during your earlier Freebie search. Dig around in **Inventory** (Ctrl-I) and **Library** files.

TRYING ON CLOTHES

♦ *Left-click* and open your **Inventory** (Ctrl-I); Locate something you want to try on.

♦ *Right-click* the file and select "**Wear**" from the pie menu that opens. Give it a moment and the clothing item then will appear on your Avatar. Notice it replaces any other item that is in the same clothing layer.

♦ An alternative method is to drag each item from your inventory onto your Avatar: Now go ahead find another clothing item and *Left-click* and *hold* the file while you *drag* it from the **Inventory** onto your Avatar. Then *release* your mouse.

♦ Now take it off. *Right-click* on the same file and *select* **Take Off** (you may be asked specifically which clothing item). If it is an attachment then you will be asked to **Detach from Yourself**.

♦ Now take something else off using your Avatar directly. *Right-click* a clothing item on your Avatar and *select* **Take Of** *or* **Detach**. If it is an Avatar minimum item, you can only **Edit** unless you *select* another file to **Wear** in your **Inventory** as a replacement in that category. Go ahead, try to put on and take off a couple of different items both directly from your Avatar and from **Inventory** (Ctrl-I).

♦ Notice that any removed clothing item remains in the same place in your **Inventory** (Ctrl-I) where it always was. Wearing it and taking it off doesn't affect its location in your **Inventory**. You can move the location in **Inventory** even if you are wearing the item.

QUICK CHANGE

♦ Let's try a faster change. *Drag* a clothing **folder** now from **Inventory** that contains an outfit set you want to wear. Go ahead and *drop it* on your Avatar for a quick change. Make sure the outfit contents are complete because using this method removes all your clothing items as a part of the process. If the **folder** contains nothing but pants then that's all you'll be seen wearing.

♦ Now find or *set up* a **Folder** with one or two clothing items in it. *Right-click* on the **folder** and *select* "**Add to Outfit**." Notice the items now appeared on you. This way you don't accidentally end off taking everything else off and accidentally ending up naked.

♦ Once the items are on, Go ahead and *right-click* that **folder** again. Select **Take Off Items**. Now they are gone, again without disturbing the rest of your outfit.

♦ These options will help you manage some fast and deft changes of your Avatar shape, skin, and outfits. It just requires a little planning and preparation to get "outfit sets" into folders so you are ready for a quick change at the spur of the moment. Never be caught with an inappropriate outfit again. You can now be packed and ready for any occasion.

Fascinating Changes

Second Life is about your own personal expression played out through your Avatar. Try different personas out, have fun with the infinite possibilities you can design. These ready made tools that are provided for creating your **Appearance** are very simple to use. You can change your chin tilt, color of your skin, size of your forehead, the length of your hair. Don't worry if it isn't perfect all at once. You can keep working on perfection, experimenting with skins and clothes, and of course do a quick change any time you want. Once you get the hang of it, you will have a full wardrobe of looks.

APPEARANCE TIPS AND HINTS:

• Make sure you are selecting a clothing item and not a box to "Wear." A common blunder is not unpacking a box of clothing and wearing the box instead. Hint: If an object has a cube icon in front of it, it will also be still in your **Objects** folder. If you can't tell if the item is "unpacked" then take it out of **Inventory** (Ctrl-I) first and look at it on the ground. A definite Newbie sighting is an Avatar wearing a box.

• If you like your **Appearance**, then gather all the items listed as **worn** and place them all in one file folder. Then make a **Copy** (Ctrl-C) of the **outfit folder** for safe keeping. Items that can be **copied** can be added over and over to different "outfits" to be used repeatedly.

• Any item in your outfit that is **no-copy** will only be moved (not copied) to the new outfit folder. The other items though will be copied. If it is a critical wardrobe element for you that you like to use repeatedly, then set it up in a separate folder to *right-click* and **Add to Outfit** whenever you change your clothes.

APPEARANCE TIPS AND HINTS: (Cont.)

• Set up Outfits to be complete with your selection of shape, skin, hair, and eyes. Then if you are experimenting with a look and decide you don't like it and want to go back to your last "look", you will have all the pieces in one place for a fast change. It happens a lot that "looks" get messed up and nine out of ten new people haven't planned for it. Don't let this happen to you!

• Any changes you make to your "look" through the **Appearance Edit** function will be saved over the file you are wearing. So, remember to **MAKE A COPY** before you start experimenting.

• Your SL account and Avatar aren't restricted to any one gender (or a gender at all). You can **Save** different outfits of any gender and switch between them whenever you like. The **Library** folder in your **Inventory** has various male and female outfits and skins to choose from. Go ahead and mix and match. Just remember when you *select* **Wear** they default a **Copy** into your **Inventory**. It's easier to control if you **Copy Library** files before using them.

• If you use a shirt made by someone else and it is modifiable and you use it as the basis for your new shirt, you won't be noted as the creator. To be the Creator you need to take off the shirt you are wearing and choose to make a new one. If a clothing item is not modifiable, you will have to take it off in order to make a new one.

• To change the shape, you are limited to the sliders available on that clothing layer. This means that you cannot choose to have transparent parts to the shirt, unless the texture you have used already has transparent sections, like a lace texture. You also can't introduce detail like collars and lapels and buttons unless these are already on the texture you have applied.

• Textures are not scaleable like textures used in Build. In the Appearance Window you are limited and will end up with mismatching seams and over or undersized pattern repeats. Some textures will work better than others but patterns need to be laid out on a template which involves using a graphics program like PhotoShop, PaintShop Pro, etc.

• Once you have made something you want to keep, click on "Save As" at the bottom of the menu, name it with something that will make you remember what it is. If you use your initials in the title it helps in locating the item and remembering it as your creation.

APPEARANCE TIPS AND HINTS: (Cont.)

- The other area where people find clothing difficult is in achieving transparent layers. There is a procedure for saving alpha layers which has to be conformed to, and then the texture has to be saved as a "tga" file type in order for it to retain its transparency. These are techniques that require the use of graphics programs. The advanced techniques will be covered in subsequent books. In this book we are concentrating on the basics.

- Hover Tips display information about land and objects, such as name, owner, permissions, and price (if for sale). If you don't see them, the hover tips may be turned off by default. Turn them on through the Menu Bar; *left-click* **View** and you have the options to *tick* **Show Tips** (Ctrl-Shift-T); **Land Tips**; and **Tips on** All Objects.

INFORMATION: APPEARANCE EDITING

Right-click on your Avatar and from the pie menu *select* **Appearance**; or from the **Edit** on the top Menu Bar *select* **Appearance**. The **Appearance Window** will then open and you'll see your Avatar spin around, so you are ready to be customized!

On the right, are thumbnail previews, *move* the slider left or right or move the numbers incrementally to see the effect. *Drag* the scroll bar *down* for more options. These are the general tools that apply to all panes in the **Appearance Window**. Don't be afraid to experiment. There is no secret formula, just learn by doing.

The left hand side of the **Appearance Window** is divided into two categories, **Body Parts** and **Clothes**. *Click* a tab on the left and a pane corresponding with the category will show.

CHANGING YOUR BODY PARTS

SHAPE
Body, Head, Eyes, Ears, Nose, Mouth, Chin, Torso, Legs, Male/Female are your choices to change or modify. Here you choose generally sizes for things like height and facial features.

INFORMATION: APPEARANCE EDITING (Cont.)

SKIN

Skin Color, Face Detail, Makeup, and Body Detail are found here. You can select to have freckles, add color to your lips, or even stamp on a daring tattoo. Speaking of tattoos, the three Tattoo boxes (gray X's if no tattoos have been applied) can be clicked to open a **Texture Picker**, similar to **Build**, additional textures can be selected and layered on your head, upper body, and lower body.

Textures for tattoos and replacement skins are often created and sold by other Residents. These are appealing because they usually have more graphic detail replicating life-like qualities that further enhance your Avatars look, i.e. more than what can only be constructed here.

HAIR

Color, Style, Eyebrows, and Facial Hair are controlled here. There's a Texture box to change the "weave" of your hair. Give it a try. *Click* the **Texture Picker** box, find and *select* any texture in your **Inventory** (Ctrl-I), and watch your hair change. Use the **Cancel** button if you don't want to keep it. Facial Hair is only offered on the "Male" selected Avatars (*click* on the Shape Button to select a Male or Female Body).

Prim and Flex Hair is sold throughout SL. It is the artful arrangements of the primitive building blocks we have been using, but in this case it is fashioned and "Flexed" (so it moves with motion) to look like hair. These pieces are assembled and sold as an "Attachment" for a unique natural look.

EYES

Just one Iris box is displayed. Again a **Texture Picker** is available to change the texture in a similar way to the Hair and Tattoo boxes. Again, many Residents have made their own eyes as upgrades for the templates offered. You will find Avatar body parts are popular items for sale in-world. There are also many freebies available to experiment with.

RANDOMIZE

This Button is also fun to try for each of the body parts. *Click* the button for some spontaneous results, you may come across something you like or may be inspired to try something totally different.

INFORMATION: APPEARANCE EDITING (Cont.)

CHANGING YOUR CLOTHING

Shirt, Pants, Shoes, Socks, Jacket, Gloves, Undershirt, Underpants, and Skirt: These are different types of clothing which all have a Fabric box (Jacket has Upper Fabric and Lower Fabric boxes) and Color/Tint to adjust the hue. Clothes without **Copy Permissions** won't show the Fabric box to protect the texture from being copied.

Each type of clothing layer has a unique set of sliders with appropriate attributes for your use in creating your own unique design. Drag each one to find out what it does. If you're not wearing anything on a certain layer, it will say "not worn" along with a **Create** button offer to develop your own. Starting with a white template, you can add Fabric and Color. Use the sliders for sizing, length, collars, and wrinkles. **Create** your clothes here from scratch.

OTHER APPEARANCE SETTINGS

At the bottom of the Appearance window are these buttons:

Take Off
This button takes off the currently selected layer of clothes. This doesn't apply to the minimum body parts like skin or eye. Body parts can only be **exchanged** and not eliminated. To "**exchange**" just find another body part of the same type (shape, skin, hair, eyes) in your **Inventory** and *double left-click* it, or *right-click* it and *select* **Wear**.

Save
Saves the current selection of body part or clothes to your **Inventory** file. Save is not offered if the item's **permission** is not modifiable (**No Mod**).

Save As
Saves a copy of the currently selected body part or clothes under new file names.

Revert
If you change your mind after making changes using the appearance sliders, you can click Revert and it changes back your setting to the original set appearance set. Note that this will not undo after a save. Also any recent exchanging of a body part or after taking off/Wear is used on clothing items.

INFORMATION: APPEARANCE EDITING (Cont.)

SAVE YOURSELF

We can't tell you to do this enough. Always save the appearances you want to keep. Anything can happen unexpectedly in SL and you can loose what you pulled together.

Make Outfit
Tick the items you want to **Save**; Type a **Folder** name; then *left-click* **Save**. Look in your **Inventory**, in the **Clothing** folder for the **New Outfit** folder you just created.

Rename Clothing To Folder Name
This checkbox is useful when making and saving a full outfit with matching items and you want a folder with the items renamed automatically. For instance, a skirt previously called "test" becomes "Pink Outfit Skirt" if the folder name is "**Pink Outfit.**" Since **No Copy** items obviously can't be duplicated, they'll just be moved to the **New Folder** after the **Make Outfit** process.

Save All
Click to save all the changes you've made. This won't create additional copies; it just updates everything you've done since opening the **Appearance Window** so your changes are applied.

Close
When you're done saving, *click* to make the **Appearance Window** go away.

Unique Self Expression

While an Avatar is thought of as a single resident, you can make additional outfit folders in **Inventory**, and if each folder is a completely different look, each can be considered as a unique Avatar. Some Residents collect Avatars for fun and self-expression. You may come across someone who's a normal looking humanoid one day, a green dragon the next and an anthropomorphic fox the day after that! Some people have extensive wardrobes and make a wide range of changes. Some Avatars change their complete look two or three times within a day. It's fascinating to just watch what people come up with next.

To wear everything in a folder and effectively change Avatars, just *drag* it from inventory onto yourself, and watch as you morph from one form to another in a few seconds! Changing clothes and bodies is so easy.

Making It in Second Life

It is possible to make clothes through the **Appearance Window**. It is also possible to import clothes using templates and texture upload for L$10 (Ctrl-U). You can create clothes in-world. These clothing items can be stored in your **Clothing** folder, they can also be structured so you can transfer and even sell them. You can easily search the Internet and try-out some textures (just be aware of any copyrights). When you **Upload** Textures (Ctrl-U) there is a L$10 charge.

If you want to use the texture for clothes, try it out first in the **Upload Window** by clicking on the drop down menu and selecting the appropriate clothing type for viewing. This can save you L$10 since clothing patterns only look good if it's laid out on a template, which is a subject that you are not quite ready for yet. Back to basics. Read the information below. It will give you insight into boxing and selling your clothes (or any product) for sale. Whether you are the Seller or the Buyer, this is how shopping works in Second Life.

INFORMATION: SEW IT AND SELL IT

Creations can easily be bought and sold in Second Life's marketplaces. The best way to sell clothing, scripts, animations, etc. is to "package" them in a box. This works great for multiple items or full outfits. Then add a Note and a Landmark for instructions and advertising. Here's how to do it:

- *Right-click* the object and select **Edit**
- *Left-click* the **General Tab**. (*click* **More>** if you don't see it.)
- *Tick* the **For Sale** Button
- Type in a price (in L$) in the space next to **For Sale**
- *Tick* on one of the following **methods** you wish to use for selling the object:

Original: Sell the object (not a copy). When a resident buys the original, that object transfers ownership.

Copy: A resident buys an exact duplicate of the object and the original is still owned by the seller.

Contents: Sell multiple items out of a box (not with the box). The Buyer receives a folder (with the same name as the Box) containing a copy of the contents (or if the contents is **No Copy** then receives the actual items).

BOXING FOR FUN

Don't stress about the look of your clothing item and box in this exercise. The purpose is to understand how you make an item and box it for transfer or sale. The box nicely packs up the clothing item, Note, and Landmark.

MAKE A PLAID TEE-SHIRT

Right-click your Avatar, and *select* **Appearance**. The **Appearance Window** opens to a list of clothing items.

To make a TEE-SHIRT, for example, begin with a *left-click* of "**shirt**." If you are wearing one, and it is modifiable, you will see the pictures for the various sliders displayed on the shirt page of the **Appearance Window**. If you see a grey page, you do not have **permission** to modify this clothing item. In this case you might have received it as a gift, picked it up in one of your freebie packs, or bought it.

If you have a shirt on, take it off (*left-click* "**Take Off**" button in the **Appearance Window**).To be the Creator on this new shirt, you have to make your own and not modify any existing shirt you might be wearing created by someone else.

Once you choose to make a new shirt, *left-click* "**Create New Shirt**" and a white un-textured shirt will show up on your Avatar. You will notice that there are two blank windows: a **Fabric** and a **Color/Tint** window. *Left-click* opens a **Texture Picker** or **Color Picker** respectively. Find a Plaid Texture in your **Library** Folder and *select* it. Do the same for the color if you want. Size the TEE-SHIRT for sleeve and shirt length, collar, fit, and wrinkles.

Now **Save** your New Shirt as "*Plaid TEE-SHIRT*". Open **Inventory** (Ctrl-I); and find the *Plaid TEE-SHIRT* in your **Clothing** folder. It should have a notation "**(worn)**" after it. Also notice the **shirt icon** designating the clothing and layer type.

You can close your **Appearance Window** and **Save all** if you want to keep the TEE-SHIRT on and keep your **Appearance** intact. Note what folder your *Plaid TEE-SHIRT* saved into. Also note where the rest of your outfit is located. You can find the pieces easily because there will be a "**(worn)**" notation after the clothing item.

PLAID TEE-SHIRT (BOXED) FOR SALE

Now let's set up the *Plaid TEE-SHIRT* in a Box to be sold for L$0 (same as "Free").

SET UP A BOX FOR SELLING YOUR TEE-SHIRT

Create a Cube (Ctrl-4) on the ground. *Right-click* and *Select* **Edit**. Rename it "**Plaid TEE-SHIRT (boxed)**" in the **General Tab** pane. Also *tick* "*Copy*" (which *un-ticks* the "**Original**" setting). This means you can sell more than one boxed Plaid TEE-SHIRT set. If you leave "**Original**" ticked, you can only sell it once. Now *tick* "**sell**" and type in the price of L$ "**0**" for your boxed Plaid TEE-SHIRT. *Click* **Textures Tab**; open the **Texture Picker**; Select the same Plaid texture and color for texturing your box (so it looks like better than the plywood default texture).

PLACE PLAID TEE-SHIRT IN THE BOX

To begin*, Left-click* the **Content Tab** to open the pane; In **Inventory**, locate your *Plaid TEE-SHIRT.* If you are still wearing it, you need to either take it off by replacing it with another Shirt for this step or *right-click* the file or make another copy in your **Inventory** so that you can Box it for sale. *Left-click*, *hold* and *drag* it onto your Cube or onto the **Content Tab** pane. Now if you want to put your Plaid TEE-SHIRT back on you can.

ADD A NOTE TO THE BOX

In the **Inventory** Window, *select* **Create**, *select* **New Note**. The "New Note" will be located in the **Notecards** Folder. *Drag* the *New Note file* onto your Box. In the **Content Tab**, *double left-click* (or *right-click* **Open**) and type in a Description and a note (anything for now). Select **Save** and close (*select* top right hand corner "**X**"). Again, *Right-click* **New Note** file in the **Content Tab**; this time *select* **Rename**. Now rename the note "**Plaid TEE-SHIRT Information.**"

ADD A LANDMARK TO THE BOX

Now in the Menu Bar select **World**; select "**Create Landmark Here.**" Close *Landmark* by selecting top right hand corner "**X**." *Drag* the top Landmark file into the **Content Tab** pane or unto the Box from your **Landmarks Inventory** Folder. The Landmark you offer would typically be your place of Business. Now *right-click* and "**Take**" your *Plaid-Shirt (boxed)* and it can now be found in your **Inventory** under the **Objects** Folder.

BOXING FOR SALE

This is how you would set up any clothing item you design "**for sale**". Your "*Plaid TEE-SHIRT (boxed)*" can be displayed for sale. When an Avatar touches it a hover box displays the name of the object; name of the Owner, and the selling price. Then when they *right-click*, the **Buy Window** opens (see *right-click*; *select* **More**; *select* **Buy** for a demonstration) and the sale can transact with the Buyer paying the requested amount and receiving the Box into **Inventory**. That's how it works. Now go ahead and *right-click* and select "**Take**" to place the Plaid TEE-SHIRT (boxed) into your Inventory.

See **Chapter 7** for more information on the **Buy** function and associated **permissions** that can be transferred in a **Sale**.

More than One Life to Live

Behind each Avatar in Second Life is a real person. Conversely, each real person is experiencing SL through their Avatar. This is one of those "once in a lifetime" chances to be whomever you want to be, project whatever you want to project, experience whatever you want to experience. For some it's a dream come true. For others, it's an extension of who they are in real life. Even for others, it's both by having a "real" Avatar and an alternate account with a "play" Avatar.

Second Life provides you with the tools to customize your Avatar in an infinite amount of ways. You can change the shape of your body, instantly swap one set of clothes for another, give yourself a tan and buff physique without the workout, and there's an assortment of features you can adjust with easy-to-use sliders. You can make yourself grotesque by bulging an eyeball or bulk up your stomach to look pregnant, you can grow a beard, have purple skin, tryout blue eyes, and even attach wings or a tail.

How you appear is how others see you, and being an Avatar you're not confined to a single look. You can edit your appearance as often as you like.

It's NOW time to get started...experiment ...create yourself!

CHAPTER 12:
SEW IN STYLE
Clothes Hog!

Flex-It!

Feel like flexing something. You know, bending it till it almost breaks. Letting it blow in the wind. Ever been in that kind of mood? In Second Life you can actually flex your objects if you want. It's as easy as ticking the Flexible Box and playing again with the numbers. Like most things in SL, experiment and learn. Flexing hair, skirts, capes, hats, and anything else you can think of is quite the fashion rage in Second Life. The fashion statement is often referred to as Prim Clothes or Flexi Clothes (or Prim Hair and Flexi-Hair). Whatever you want to call it, but let's have some fun, and give it a go.

EXERCISE 12: FLEXI-CREATIONS

CREATE AND TEST FLEXI-PRIMS

- ◆ **Create** a Cube (Ctrl-4) on the ground. *Left-click* the **Features Tab** (if you don't see it then *click* the "**More**" Button. Then *tick* **Flexible Path**. Now increase the number next to **Wind to X**. Your Cube should be slumped over.

- ◆ **Make it taller.** *Click* on the **Object Tab** and set your Cube **Size of Z to 10** (or Ctrl-Shift and *drag* the blue sizing box to stretch it as far as it will go). This causes the stretched-out cube to appear stretching itself out on the ground.

- ◆ **Move it around.** Go ahead and check out how it responds when you move it around (in **Edit** *left-click* and *drag* on the arrows).

- ◆ **Change Shapes:** In the **Object Tab**, *click* on the **Building Block** drop-down menu and *select* **Prism**.

- ◆ **Test Softness:** Return to the **Features Tab** and **lower Softness to 0**, then **raise the softness to 3**. Notice what happens?

- ◆ **Test Gravity.** Try a positive number and then a negative number.

- ◆ **Try all the Settings.** Go ahead and try other settings and combinations to see the effects. Now you're getting the idea on how flexi flexible actually is. When you're done, just **delete** (key) the object while it is in **Edit** mode.

Blowing in the Wind

In Second Life you can actually create the real life equivalent of your perfect serene scene. Pick one out of memory and you can actually recreate it in Second Life. Imagine yourself rocking softly in a Hammock, surrounded by gently rustling palm trees, ocean waves lapping the beach, the fire of the tiki lights fluttering, and the dry palms on the palapa umbrella shifting in the wind. Ahhhh...so relaxing. It's great to have flexibility!

INFORMATION: FLEXIBLE DETAILS

The Flexible Path settings in the **Features Tab** include:

Softness: This setting is from 0 to 3 and only in whole numbers. If the softness is set at 0, then it's akin to an uncooked noodle. Set it to 3 and it resembles a cooked noodle. There is a maximum of 6 segments being affected on a Prim. All segments are affected when softness is set at 3.

Tension: Think of this as a flexible object's "backbone ". A 0.0 setting has no backbone so it becomes limp. The 10.0 setting is the equivalent in firmness to a solid board.

Drag: This setting applies air friction to a flexible Prim. A low number makes the Prim wiggle wildly. A higher number increasing it towards the maximum of 10.0 affects the Prim making it look like it's reacting in slow motion (you will see it gently swaying).

Gravity: This is a downward force. Think of a heavy object in real life. It won't stay in the air, it will sink through floors until it hits the ground (especially if you place the object on the floor without it having a physical setting). A negative number will actually make the Prim defy gravity and float upward.

Wind: There is wind in Second Life. A higher number on your Prim for wind increases the affect wind has on the flexible Prim. Compare a leaf fluttering around to a ball's movement from wind. The affect is in the wind.

Prim Boxes, Cylinders, and Prisms can have a flexible path. Flexible objects are a client-side effect, which means it can noticeably slow down performance on your computer, but won't slow down the server. Flexible objects can be temporarily disabled by un-checking Flex Objects on the **Debug** menu (Ctrl-Alt-D). Look for "**Client**" to appear in the Menu Bar [Client: Rendering: Features: Flexible Objects (Ctrl-Alt-9)]

Getting Attached

The Appearance of your Avatar is easily designed through the **Appearance Window**. Looks and styles can be further improved by importing textures that have been enhanced with details like buttons, bows, creases, collars, and cuffs through graphic programs and templates. In addition, accessories designed from Prims can be "**Attached**" to more than 30 places on your Avatar. Using the **Build** tools (B), these accessories can be created to respond to movement, wind, and gravity. Attachments can provide for a unique and more realistic presentation.

Since Avatars come in all shapes and sizes, adjusting something like the fit of glasses, bracelet, or a necklace is easier when it's already attached. Some Residents use posing stands which freezes the Avatar into a position for more precise adjustments. This is especially useful when customizing something complex, such as hair pieces.

HUDs (Head's Up Display) are also attachments, but attach to 8 places on your screen. They are typically used for displays and controls. For example, a **HUD** might be set up to display a dashboard to make it easier for you to maneuver a vehicle. You might choose to buy and attach an animation **HUD** that allows you to easily control gestures and animations on your Avatar. Other **HUDs** might display racing scores, cards in a tournament poker game, make reading a book easier, or reviewing a photo album. They are used as a personal overlay for your benefit only. It doesn't have to be scripted, but **HUDs** typically are designed by the Residents who create them in SL to be interactive.

Though any object can be worn as an **Avatar Attachment** or a **HUD attachment**, it is not recommended to attach a couch to your hip, since it would be considered strange. If you attach a scripted door as a **HUD** it will open and close on touch, but you have to ask yourself, is it practical?

INFORMATION: ATTACHMENTS

AVATAR ATTACHMENTS

An **Attachment** is an object that is attached to an Avatar. There are numerous **attachment points** to choose from. Whatever can be attached can be detached or dropped as well.

An object is affixed via the **attach** command (*right-click* the object for the pie menu or *right-click* the **Inventory** file for the option menu). Attach options are listed (for example, skull, chin, left hand, foot, etc.)

To detach an object, *right-click* it and two options become available:

> **Detach:** Releases the object from the Avatar and places it into **Inventory**.

> **Drop:** The object is released from the Avatar and falls to the ground next to your Avatar.

INFORMATION: ATTACHMENTS (Cont.)

Prim objects that have been created by other residents include shoes, jewelry, hair, hats, masks, glasses, wings, watches, and other items. Some Prim objects are 'scripted" so they create their own action or affect. Jewelry has bling, watches keep real time, shoes can animate your Avatar's walk.

Making objects from Prims allows for more dimensions and detail then otherwise would be achieved through the Appearance window. Complete Avatars have also been constructed out of Prims. The furry creatures that are seen in communities like Lusk are examples of inhabitants who have perfected their creatures through the extensive use of Prim attachments to create a particular effect. Look also for Winged Avatars, some of these residents have gone to great length creating these beautiful looks. As a result, you will find "groups", "regions", and themed communities within Second Life.

HUD ATTACHMENT

Heads-Up Displays (HUDs) in Second Life are attachment points located on your computer screen. There are 8 **HUD** points available to you. These are NOT attachment points on the body. These displays can only be seen by you. Other residents may also be viewing **HUDs** on their screens and you can't view them.

Attach HUD:

- *Right-click* Object
- *Select* **More>**
- *Select* **Attach HUD**
- *Select* one of the following positions noted in the pie menu: **Top, Top Right, Top Left, Center, Center 2, Bottom Left, Bottom Right**, and **Bottom.**

ADDITIONAL HUD ATTACHMENT OPTIONS

Right-click the object while it is attached to your computer screen and the pie menu offers 3 options:

Detach: Releases the object from your computer screen and places it into **Inventory**.

INFORMATION: ATTACHMENTS (Cont.)

Edit: This is the regular **Edit** tool. All the same functions can be used on the object while attached as a **HUD** to your computer screen. You can resize it, change texture, or even rotate the object's position or *drag* it to a different part of the screen.

Drop: The object is released from the Avatar and falls to the ground next to your Avatar. It does not go to your **Inventory**.

If your **HUD** attached object is difficult to see, you can use your mouse's scroll wheel or *click* **Focus** (Ctrl-1) in the **Edit** pane. Then *drag* the Zoom slider for zooming in and out. At anytime press the esc key to reset the view. Notice that the attached object still stays in place, even as you move your cursor or your Avatar around. If you don't want to see the **HUD** but still wish to keep it attached, then change the setting in the Menu Bar. *Left-click* **View**; *tick* or *un-tick* **Show HUD Attachments** (Alt-Shift-H).

SHORTCUT COMMANDS:

Show Tips*	Ctrl-Shift-T
Focus	Ctrl-1
Reset View	Esc (key)
Show HUD Attachments*	Alt-Shift-H
Debug Menu*	Ctrl-Alt-D

Toggles on and off

Get Attached

Avatar attachments (clothes, hair, hats, capes, etc.) are often designed using the Flexible Path feature because when you move, the natural look you project is definitely noticed. Typically you will attach accessories to your Avatar similar to how you would use accessories in real life. The first impression you create will say volumes about you. What would you think if you met an Avatar wearing a box on his head? What would you think if you saw an elaborately winged Avatar with flowing hair and a sparkling gown? What about a green dragon that blows friendly fire and smoke? Would you say Imaginative? Even talented and creative are words that come to mind.

It's interesting to just people-watch in Second Life. Between people watching and window shopping, you will begin to form ideas about what you would like to do in designing the appearance of your Avatar. Now that you understand the flexibility of attachments, pat yourself on the back. You've come a long way.

PRIM ATTACHMENT TIPS AND HINTS:

- You can attach more than one object to your screen. You can NOT attach more than one object to the same **HUD** position.

- **HUDs** can be attached by *right-clicking* the object or by *right-clicking* the file in your **Inventory** and *selecting* **Attach HUD**.

- To attach an object from your **Inventory** (Ctrl-I), *right-click* the object in your **Inventory** and choose **Wear**

- You can attach more than one object to your Avatar, but you can NOT attach more than one object to the SAME Avatar body position. For example you can't attach 2 objects to the right hand.

- If you try to attach two items to the same point, you will be asked if you want to replace the object attached there with the new one.

- Objects can be attached directly to the body by *right-clicking* the item in your **Inventory** and *selecting* **Attach**, and choosing a body location.

- Lost some objects, or not sure what items are yours? Open the **mini-map** by *left-clicking* its Button on the Button Bar. Items that are displayed on the map in blue have you listed as the owner. *Right-click* the map when it's open and options for zooming in or out are available to you.

- To detach an object from your Avatar, you have two options: *Right-click* the attachment and choose **Detach** or, *right-click* the object in **Inventory** and choose **Detach from Yourself**.

- Easily find your attached object(s) within your **Inventory** by using the Search for "**worn.**" This will show all clothing items, body parts and attachments that you're currently wearing.

- Flexible objects can't be **Physical**. However, they are **Phantom**, which means you can walk through them. If you Link them to other objects, then the entire linked object becomes phantom.

PRIM ATTACHMENT TIPS AND HINTS: (Cont.)

- When using the **Flexible Path** setting you can pre view how it responds by simply moving it around.

- Avatar attachments are anchored to the point on your body that you attached it to. These attachments go wherever you go.

- Use the **Build** Tool to **Edit** attachments. You can *right-click* the object and choose **Edit** even while you are wearing the attachment. This is useful for correctly positioning an attachment.

- When Editing an attachment, the attach point may limit how far you can move the item.

- If you *right-click* an attachment on your Avatar and **Edit** it, you won't see general info such as its name and permissions. You can still view them in your **Inventory** (Ctrl-I); *right-click* on the file and then *select* **Properties**.

- You can't **Link** (Ctrl-L) and **Unlink** (Ctrl-Shift-L) Prims while they are attached to a **HUD** or Avatar. If you need to do this, *right-click* the attachment and **Drop** it so you can **Edit** it on the ground.

- Multiple objects can't be attached to a single point so make sure you **Link** everything you want, then attach as one object.

- When editing avatar attachments with multiple parts, place (not attach) the object against your avatar. (Un-link it for editing). When done, then link it and attach. Posing stands are also helpful for positioning your avatar into a frozen stance for editing multiple parts.

- **Avatar** and **HUD Attachments** will be automatically saved to attach to the last point it was attached to. Any change in positioning done by *right-clicking* it to **Edit** will be saved.

- Experiment with Editing Attachments. When you do, it is **RECOMMENDED** that you **copy** the item first (if it is copyable) so if something goes wrong you don't lose the original. To **Copy**, *right-click* the item's file name in **Inventory**, select **Copy** (Ctrl-C), and *right-click* it again in the same folder and *select* **Paste** (Ctrl-V). If the object is also modifiable, then rename it. For example, "Glasses" becomes "Glasses (Backup)".

HUD ATTACHMENTS TO TRY

If your World looks dark, don't forget to turn on the Noon lights (Ctrl-Shift-Y) so you can see.

FRAMED ROSE COLORED HUD

- **Create** a Cube (Ctrl-4) on the ground

- In the **Object Tab**, set **Hollow = 90**; set **Rotation (degrees) Y = 90**

- In the **Texture Tab** use the **Color Picker Window** to change color to **black**.

- *Right-click* object and *select* **More>**

- *select* **Attach HUD**; *select* **Center 2**.

- **Create** another Cube (Ctrl-4) on the ground

- In the **Texture Tab** pane, select the **Texture Picker** and select **Blank**

- Then *select* the **Color Picker Window** and *select* a **red**

- *Set* **Transparent = 50**

- *Right-click* object and *select* **More>**

- *select* **Attach HUD**; *select* **Center**

Notice what happens. The frame centers on your screen, and then the transparent "red transparent box" centers with it. **Focus** (Ctrl-1) and you can change the size view of the **HUD**. Now turn off the **HUD Attachment** (Ctrl-Shift-H) and then toggle it back on (Ctrl-Shift-H). *Right-click* the objects and *select* **Drop**. Then *right-click* and *select* **Delete** so it does not add to your **Inventory**. Now you have the idea.

EXPLORE: FOR THE ADVENTUROUS AVATAR

Already you've come a long way. You should be pretty proud of yourself now. You're developing your own signature, exploring the world, and you should be basically enjoying yourself. This book merely scratches the surface of what SL is all about. At this point, here are a few more things to try out and even explore.

GO WINDOW SHOPPING

You are not ready to design your own clothes beyond the Appearance Window. But it is a good idea to go window shopping to see what fellow residents are developing. If you have a little money you might consider buying a "look" now while you are still working on building skill and knowledge. In the meantime, window shop, collect more freebies, experiment with putting clothing items together. Try on hair, skins, body shapes, eyes, tattoos and anything else you can find. Gather intelligence on how things are done in SL and use this time to determine where your own interests lie.

Avatar Appearance Categories to Look for When Exploring:

Flexi-Hair (Prim Hair)	Jewelry and Watches
Avatar Accessories	Masks
Armor	Wings
Canes, Staves, and Wands	Avatars
Furry Creatures	Skins and Tattoos
Handbags, Backpacks, and Brief Cases	Makeup and Nails
Hats, Belts, and Glasses	Speed and Flying Assistance
HUD Attachments	Animals and Creatures
Robots, Monsters, Sci-Fi Bodies	Animations

Excellent places to explore are the two largest Exchanges:

- SL Exchange Marketplace: www.SLExchange.com
- SL Boutique: www.SLBoutique.com

If you want to shop the exchanges, just open your browser and follow the web site instructions to register. These exchanges give you a quick look of the range of innovative products available in Second Life. It doesn't cost to look.

Shop Till You Drop

Interested in buying products? Then follow the instructions on the exchanges listed above, their websites will direct you on setting up an account and registering your Avatar. You will be instructed to visit their in-world ATM by clicking on a listed ATM location which populates your SL Map for teleporting directly to a terminal. This creates the connection between your account and your Avatar. Then all you have to do is click on the terminal, deposit some Linden dollars through your Avatar when you are in SL or by credit card directly on the website. Now you have an account on-line with direct product delivery to your Inventory folder in-world. It's that easy.

In the meantime, use the exchanges to Window Shop. SL Exchange alone has over 40,000 apparel items listed. Both exchanges offer tons of Free Stuff too. When you are ready to sell product, these exchanges are excellent places to advertise.

It's All About You

Everything you do is experienced through your Avatar. The people you will meet relate to your Avatar. You should now understand why everyone takes a great deal of personal interest in developing their Avatar's personality through their Appearance, Attachments, and Profile. We covered Appearance and Attachments. Next will be your Profile.

CHAPTER 13:
CAPTURE THE MOMENT
Just Picture This

Photo Opportunity

At this point you should have at least changed your look somewhat from the template Avatar you chose upon joining Second Life. This is a good time to memorialize how you look by taking a picture as the first start to your personal SL photo album. As we said in the beginning, you will create and re-create yourself at least 5 to 10 times over. Some of these early pictures will eventually be cherished. So this is a good time to start learning how to take Snapshots in Second Life. Not only will you want to photograph yourself, but you will also want to photograph some of your builds or even other people's builds to use them for reference.

CONSTRUCT A PHOTO STUDIO

CREATE A FLOOR AND BACK WALL

- **Create** a Cube (Ctrl-4) on the ground
- On the **Object Tab** pane, Re-size the Cube: **X=10.0m; Y=10.0m; Z=0.100**
- Make a **Copy** (Shift-*hold* and *drag* upward on the Z arrow until you have two parallel cubes that are flat). Let's call them platforms.
- On the **Object Tab** pane of the floating Platform (call it #2) change this Cube to: Y_2 **Rotation = 90 degrees**

"L" SHAPE IT

- Using your eye (doesn't have to be Prim perfect), go ahead and *left-click drag* the **blue Z arrow** up so that the bottom edge of the flat cube is perpendicular to the flat floor piece
- Use the **Y arrow** and drag it (or push it) to an end of the floor platform piece. You are trying to position one flat Cube piece as a back wall with the other positioned as the floor. Achieving an "L" shape using these two Prims.

Double the size of your platform by using the Copy function in Edit or Shift-dragging out another back wall and another floor platform. Essentially doubling the size. Just align them to eliminate gaps.

CONSTRUCT A PHOTO STUDIO (Cont.)

COLOR IT

- Once the "L" is formed then in the Edit mode, open the **Texture Tab**

- Open the **Texture Picker** and *select* "**Blank**"

- Open the **Color Picker** and *select* White

- Then make sure you *tick* the **Full Bright** feature

- Apply the same texture and color for the back as well as the floor of your Photo Backdrop. The white (or black) make for an interesting affect in snapshots.

SCENE IT

Alternatively you can change the backdrop texture of your platform to one of the Scenes found in your Library, look in the Snapshots folder. You can also retexture the Floor with a Grass Texture also from your Library Folder.

Now let's use it to take some awesome pictures.

EXERCISE 13: TAKING PICTURES

When you open Snapshot it can be confusing. Be patient and follow through the exercise. Save your pictures **Free** to your computer for viewing. Once you decide on a picture that you like; *select* **File** in the Menu Bar and click **Upload Image (L$10)** to bring it into your **Inventory**. It will be placed in the **Textures** folder.

RESET SNAPSHOT PREVIEW

- *Left-click* the "**Snapshot**" button (Ctrl-Shift-S) at the bottom of your screen. You might see a flash as it opens to the **Snapshot Preview** pane. What you'll also notice is that the **User Interface** (Menu Bar, Buttons, Windows, etc.) has disappeared and the world and your Avatar may appear "frozen."

- In **Snapshot Preview** (Ctrl-Shift-S) if the **Freeze Frame** is ticked your cursor becomes a magnifying glass. *Left-click* and *drag* to change the view or angle of your camera shot. At this point, when the magnifier is moved, your screen will show a visual effect of dropping away a photo and then your **User Interface (UI)** will reappear.

- This all can look confusing at first. So reset the Snapshot pane by *un-ticking* everything listed there that you can, including "**Freeze frame**" and auto **Snap-shot**. Now we can choose the settings below and start the photo shoot.

TAKE A STUDIO PICTURE

♦ *Tick* Save **Snapshot to hard drive**; *tick* **Keep open after saving.**

♦ Position yourself on the ***Photo Backdrop Platform*** (see build instructions above). Walk to the center and turn so the backdrop wall is behind you (you won't see the backdrop because you are looking from behind your Avatar)

♦ With the **Snapshot Preview** open (Ctrl-Shift-S), use your cursor (*left-click hold*) with your mouse and change the angle of your camera so that you see the front of your Avatar with the white backdrop behind.

♦ Focus in on your Avatar so that your entire computer screen is filled with the white photo platform with your Avatar framed in the center of your screen.

♦ Now press Update Snapshot and your picture will appear in a view screen. If you don't like the image, then try again...and again...and again. You will soon get the hang of it.

♦ Once you capture a snapshot that you like, *left-click* the **Save** Button. A save dialog box will appear.

♦ Choose a location on your Computer to save your snapshot(s). Set up a New Folder and label it "**My SL Photos**" Then choose a filename for the photo you are saving. **IMPORTANT:** You won't be prompted for a filename again during this Second Life session, so make sure you pick a name that will help you remember this photo series.

TAKE A PICTURE ON LOCATION

♦ Take some snapshots at various locations around Second Life. Search for some elaborate Second Life builds that appeal to you (check the Appendix for **Explore Recommendations** for ideas).

♦ Some properties and malls have photo studio set-ups available with posing balls. Search to see if you can find them. Also check your Freebie stuff and see if you had picked up any posing balls. Add them to your Photo Studio set-up and take some more pictures.

SEND AN EMAIL

♦ In **Snapshot Preview** (Ctrl-Shift-S) *tick* "**Send a postcard.**" Find either a good photo opportunity location, or use your Photo Studio set-up.

♦ *Slide* the **Image Quality to 0**; then *click* "**Update Snapshot**". The quality should look poor. Now *slide* **Image Quality to 75**; *click* "Update Snapshot" again. That should be much better. Now choose a satisfactory setting between quality and size.

♦ Select **Show interface in snapshot** and take another picture. See the Menu Bar and Buttons. Don't **Discard**, just *click* **Update Snapshot** and it will replace the last picture without having to choose **Save** or **Discard**.

♦ Take a picture the way you want and email it to yourself, and then take another and send it to a friend.

INFORMATION: SNAPSHOT PREVIEW
"What would you like to do?"

OPTIONS

Send a postcard: An easy way to share snapshots with friends using email, and it's free.

Image Quality (Slider): Postcard photos are compressed and saved in a **JPEG** format. This reduction keeps email boxes from clogging up. Depending on your slider setting, you may see that the detail quality is less.

Upload a snapshot: This feature allows you to take a picture and immediately save it to your **Inventory** under the **Photo Album** folder as a file titled "Snapshot". It's not noted but you will be charged L$10. When it charges you, it will prompt you for permission to take L$10.

Save snapshot to hard drive: Saves the snapshot directly to your computer with no charge. Good for saving and viewing before spending the L$10 to upload it to your Inventory.

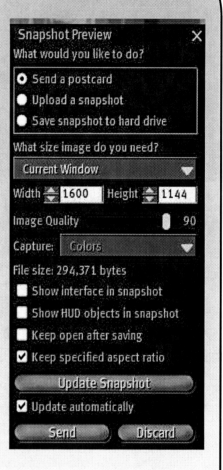

ADDITIONAL OPTIONS

What size image do you need? A size of 1280x1024 is standard, but you can change the dimensions.

Current Window: Indicates that the screen display reflects the setting input. A Larger (file) size will have more detail, but requires more memory. High resolution images will freeze your computer for awhile to process.

Colors: A drop down menu offers advanced settings. Keep in on Colors for regular shots.

> **Depth:** gives the per-pixel depth information of the scene.

> **Object Id:** Gives a unique color ID to each SL object. This ID is used to create mattes and other advanced processing of the photo in programs like Photoshop. The retro green-and-blue effect which displays can be used for artistic expressions.

INFORMATION: SNAPSHOT PREVIEW (Cont.)
"What would you like to do?"

Show interface in snapshot: The **User Interface (UI)** is the Menu Bar, Button Bar, Windows, Pie Menus, and Panes that change things in SL. By checking this box, the **UI** will show up in screenshots, which can be useful for making tutorials, reporting bugs and abuses, etc.

Show HUD objects in snapshot: The **Heads-Up Displays (HUDs)** can GET in the way of photos so you have the option to select showing them in your photo or hiding them.

Keep open after saving: This keeps the **Snapshot Preview** open after you save. This feature is very useful when you want to take multiple pictures. Then save them on your computer for review and selection later.

Keep specified aspect ratio: Allows you to crop the photo for a portrait or letterbox cut. When ticked, white bars appear showing the actual area being captured, and the rest of the screen is dimmed out. Good when selecting an odd aspect ratio (like 1228 x 500) so the picture isn't distorted unnaturally.

Update automatically: Any changes in options that are made are applied immediately when this box is checked.

Update Snapshot: Optional button to manually apply new settings when **Update automatically** isn't checked.

Save: Keep this snapshot and send it to file, or to trigger the Buy for uploading it to Inventory.

Discard: Click on Discard if you don't want to **Save** or don't wish to proceed with upload. The snapshot is discarded.

Screening Appeal

Second Life makes taking screenshots easy. Snap photos of yourself, your builds, people you meet, friends, interesting places and things. Save pictures free to your own computer's hard drive or for L$10 to your **Inventory** (Ctrl-I). It's the same as using the **Upload Image** (Ctrl-U) feature under **File**, the only difference is that it is labeled as a snapshot instead of a texture (but is essentially the same thing).

SHORTCUT COMMANDS:

Take Snapshot	Ctrl-Shift-S
Snapshot to Disk	Ctrl-`
Upload Image (L$10)	Ctl-U
View	Alt-*move mouse*
Pan	Ctrl-Alt *move mouse*
Start/Stop Movie to Disk	Ctrl-Shift-A

PHOTO TIPS AND HINTS:

- To take a snapshot without the Snapshot Preview coming up, you can just go to the **File** menu *select* **Save snapshot to hard drive** or use Ctrl-` as a shortcut (The ` key is usually located next to 1 and above Tab on your keyboard). This way you can take and save several snapshots of something quickly and easily. When you do, your Avatar will motion up to their face signaling the taking of a photo.

- Once you decide on the photo you like, use the **Upload Image** (Ctrl-U) tool in the **File** menu to upload your best shots to Second Life. You don't pay for shots you don't want, and you have time to sort through them later.

- If you use **Send a postcard** and your snapshot size is too big "File size" will be in red and you won't be able to send it. You will have to either adjust your photo size or the image quality.

- In "Upload a snapshot" mode it doesn't matter the size, it will default to a small (128x128), medium (256x256), or large (512x512) dimension. For textures, using Upload Image, they will be uploaded to the nearest power of two. For example, 128, 256, 512, 1024. So if you upload something that's 218 x 540, it will upload as 256 x 512.

- Keep in mind that after changing an option, you won't see the effect immediately unless you update the snapshot. To do this, just press the "**Update Snapshot**" button. There's also a handy "**Update automatically**" checkbox which detects when there's changes.

- If the **Snapshot Preview** Window is blocking your view, *left-click* the top of the pane, *hold* and *drag* it anywhere on your screen to get it out of your way.

PHOTO TIPS AND HINTS:

- Once you **Upload a snapshot** and it is saved into your **Photo Album** in you **Inventory** (Ctrl-I), *right-click* the file and rename it. The **Snapshot Preview** window automatically saves it as snapshot.

- When you **Save snapshot to hard drive** the first time in a session, a window indicating the location and filename will appear. Whatever location and file name you select at this juncture, will be used throughout the session and can not be changed.

- Your snapshot file will be saved on your computer with the first name you specified plus an incremental number sequence assigned at the end. The default name is "Snapshot" if you don't assign it. (For example: Snapshot_001.bmp ; Snapshot_002.bmp,....)

Machine Cinema

You've learned how simple it is to take photos in Second Life. The natural progression from photos is the making of movies. Linden Lab not only provided the built-in tools for taking snapshots, but also comparable tools for video. A movie made in the Second Life world is called Machinima (muh-sheen-eh-mah). It's considered a new form of filmmaking. It's the making of films using computer game technology in a virtual reality environment. With Second Life there is no need for expensive camera equipment, or spending months painstakingly learning how to use expensive 3D graphic packages. Create using Machinima by using Avatars to act in-world. The movie can be script driven or it can be recorded real time.

By combining the techniques of filmmaking, animation production and the technology of real-time 3D game engines, Machinima makes for a very cost- and time-efficient way to produce films, with a large amount of creative control. Use Machinima to simply capture a moment, to see what you can do, or more seriously pursue commercial endeavors. Machinima's popularity is growing with examples emerging in film production, documentaries, training programs, use in product marketing and artistic masterpieces. Try your hand at Machinima by using the built in Movie feature provided. *Select* **File** from the Menu Bar and *click* **Start/Stop Movie to Disk** (or Ctrl-Shift-A) and also **Camera Controls** in the **View** menu. At some point give it a try. Watch for further exploration of this topic in a more advanced Book on Second Life.

Using the **Snapshot** Tool (Ctrl-Shift-S), let's see what you can really do. Participate in the following Photo Journey Challenge. This is a contest worth entering even just for the fun of it.

ENTER TO WIN
PHOTO JOURNEY CHALLENGE (PG)

You have the hang of SL photography, so let's see what you can do with your new found talent. Take our Photo Journey Challenge. It combines Photography with Exploration. Don't rush. Spend time searching around Second Life to find that Perfect Subject to photograph. We are giving Linden Dollars away monthly to the best entries. Plus if you win, your photo essay will be published and put on display at the **Photo-Art Gallery** in **Taesot (169,47,117).** As a winner, we will also send you your own published edition of your photos with the copy and transfer permissions. Now let's have some fun!

INSTRUCTIONS*:
Below are 9 photo challenges. The goal is to be creative both with the subject as well as the photography. Select your best shots. Once you've collected them:

   1. **Number the Files:** Following the numbers in category list below.

   2. **Provide Full Permissions:** copy/transfer/modify

   3. **Box the files:** Place files into a Cube (with full permissions)

   4. **Deliver it**: to the **Photo-Art Gallery** in **Taesot**. (169, 47, 117)

This is also part of the **Quick Flight Activity Challenge** that can be found in the Appendix. **Questions? IM: Reada Dailey. Categories are as follows (but use your imagination).**

Photo Journal Categories:

   1. **Unique You: (Your best self-portrait photo of your Avatar)**

   2. **Creative Capture: (Fury, Winged, or other Creature)**

   3. **Primnimal Primate: (Non-Avatar Prim Animal)**

   4. **Wondrous Water: (Water element or scene)**

   5. **Fire Fantasy: (Fire or Particle Display)**

   6. **Bountiful Build: (Any Absolutely Awesome Build)**

   7. **Avatar Accessory: (A Flexi or otherwise Fashion Statement)**

   8. **Artistic Arrangement: (Use your creative eye to capture a moment)**

   9. **Awesome Activity: (Catch an Action in SL)**

Entries will only be considered if they are properly numbered (not necessary to use the subject title), boxed, and proper permissions provided. The photos can be submitted as Texture or Snapshot files. Rating: PG. Judged by the v3image staff. No deadline Date, v3image retains the right to cancel the contest at anytime. Minimum of 3 NEW entries must be submitted before a month is announced as a Contest Month. Non-winner entries roll over as entries in subsequent designated Contest Months. Only one entry per Avatar will be accepted. All submittals become the property of v3image. Photos will not be returned.

CHAPTER 14:
PROFILING FUN
Groupies Do Rock

Who are you?

Remember you get to choose who you are, how you look, where you live, and what you do in Second Life. A good part of defining yourself is the information you share publicly. Through your **Profile**, you communicate and further project your image.

Your name and born date is the only information you can't change, although there is a lot of information you can add. Place a picture and information about your first and second lives. List your interests and your Groups. Add a web-profile, favorite picks (places) and a partner. Collect and give ratings. Even get creative and subvert the Picks to show your favorite people.

A Profile for your Avatar is important. People look at them, they provide information (even by the lack of a profile) and it all creates an impression. It's your life, and defining it is a big part of the attraction found in Second Life.

INFORMATION: PROFILE WINDOW

There are 7 Profile Tabs:

| 2nd Life | Web | Interests | Picks | Classified | 1st Life | My Notes |

TABS: *Right-click* your Avatar and *select* Profile from the pie menu. The **Profile** Window shows the tabs with the following information:

2nd LIFE (References your SL persona)

Name: This is your Avatar's name. It cannot be altered.

Photo: Upload an image by left-clicking on the Photo square, a **Texture Picker** window opens. Typically the photo is of yourself or something in reference to you.

Online: Indicates whether you are in-world at that moment.

Born: The date you initially received your Avatar and started your account

Account: Type of membership account held (reflects if you signed up with a payment card (credit/PayPal)

Partner: Whether you established a partner in Second Life. It's similar to being married in real life. Partnership costs L$10 and Divorce is L$25 if you break up later. Send your proposal through the Second Life website under the Community Menu.

Ratings: People can pay L$25 per rating point; the points are for positive recognition for your **Behavior**, **Appearance**, and **Building** Skills. **Given** represents the rating points you issued to others.

Groups: This is a list of the organizations that you have joined in Second Life.

About: Your creative write-up, typically about yourself, but can be anything you want to communicate to the other residents.

Give item: If you want to send an item to a resident you drag it and drop it in this space.

Publish on the web: Selecting this option allows Linden Lab to publish your name, image, and About text on the Second Life web site.

INFORMATION: PROFILE WINDOW (Cont.)

WEB: If you have a personal web page or other web page you want to share with residents when they open your Profile, then type the URL for it here. You then have the following options:

Open: Option to view the URL in an external web browser.

Load: Option to view the URL in the embedded Browser

Automatically Load Web Profiles: If checked it automatically loads in the embedded browser.

INTERESTS: Add pre-designated categories of information and interest for yourself.

I want to: Options include: **Build, Group, Explore, Buy, Meet, Sell, Be Hired,** and **Hire.** Plus space for your own comments is available.

Skills: List your experience. Options include: **Textures, Modeling, Architecture, Scripting, Event Planning,** and **Custom Characters.** Plus space for your own comments is available.

Languages: This space allows you to list the languages that you speak.

PICKS: Tell everyone about your favorite places in Second Life.

New: Set up a location you want to tell everyone about. This button will initially populate the location picture and description as the default. You can override the populated fields with your own choice of picture, title, and description.

Delete: If you want to delete one of the location picks.

Picture: Use the Texture Picker to place your favorite picture of the Pick.

Title Box: Title your Pick for the Tab and Picture.

Description Box: Explain your Pick in your own words.

Teleport: Use this to teleport to the location.

Show on Map: Populates the World Map with the coordinates and shows the location.

Set Location: You have to be at the location to set the location.

INFORMATION: PROFILE WINDOW (Cont.)

CLASSIFIEDS: Ads that are placed by you are composed and recorded here. Similar to the Picks pane, you override the picture, title, and description. Location is set to where you are located. Once you decide to place the ad, a minimum of L$50 is required for a week in the **Classified Tab** on the **Search** Menu (Ctrl-F). Set your weekly classified payment higher and the classified display appears higher on the search results.

1ST LIFE: Space set aside for you to write about your life in Real Life if you choose. There is space for a Photo and a personalized write-up.

MY NOTES: Your notes. Every Avatar has this tab set up for others to use. Good for keeping track of information, deals, impressions, etc. Only you can see these notes (not them or anyone else). You are able to write in on this tab for any of the residents you meet so it is a convenient reference for you at any time.

Profiling Yourself

Now that you have learned to use the Appearance Window and Attachments for creating your own unique look for your Avatar, it's time to define yourself through your **Profile**. Remember in Chapter 3 how you learned to *right-click* on Avatars to open their **Profile** and learn about them (For example, when they were born). Now it's time to take a closer look at your **Profile Window** and define it for you and your Avatar.

EXERCISE 14: CREATING PROFILES

Right-click on your Avatar and *select* **Profiles** from the Pie Menu

PROFILE YOURSELF
Personalize your **Profile** by starting with the 2nd **Life** Tab

- ♦ Take your best self-portrait from Chapter 13 and Upload it from your hard drive (Ctrl-U). Pay the L$10, it's worth it. If you don't have the money, then for now, *left-click* the gray box to open the Texture Picker and *select* one of the Snapshots in your **Library**. Find them in the **Photo Album** folder.

◆ Type in something using the "**About**". You can always change it later. One way to get rid of that "Newbie" status is to fill in your **Profile**. Try to be a little creative. (See Ralph Wolf's **Profile** screen below as Ralph Kearby).

◆ Need some ideas? If you see Avatars around you, *right-click* and open their **Profiles** to get some examples and ideas on what everyone is doing. Pay special attention to the **Profiles** of the older residents.

◆ Also, *right-click* on objects that you are impressed with and select **Edit**. Note the name listed for the Creator of that object. Next to the Creator's name is a **Profile** Button. *Click* to open their **Profile** and see how they define themselves in the **2nd Life Tab**.

◆ Look-up some of the Linden employees by using the **Search** Tool (Ctrl-F). Just type in "**Linden**" using the **People Tab**. Pick a few and page through the Tabs in their **Profile**. You definitely will get see different approaches and more ideas.

JOIN A GROUP

Groups are another way that you define yourself. It's also an excellent way to get involved.

◆ Find a couple of groups that may interest. Best way to search for a group is by looking at the **Groups** other residents have joined.

◆ Open a resident's **Profile** to the **2nd Life Tab**. See their Groups list, *double left- click* on a **Group** that sounds interesting to you. If you want to join it, then press the join button in the middle of the **Group Information Window** that displays.

◆ Most of the **Groups** don't cost to join. You can always leave the group later. So join a bunch of groups for now and fill up your **Profile**. More on **Groups** later.

◆ Look for "**Quick Flight Book Group**" in the **Search** Tool (Ctrl-F), **Groups Tab** and join us.

SET UP YOUR PICKS

If you have some favorite places that you have found, then set them up in your **Picks Tab**.

◆ Since you have found a Sandbox for building, go ahead and set that location up in your **Picks Tab**.

◆ If you are not in the Sandbox now, **Teleport** to it by either using the **Search** Tool (Ctrl-F), Finding the **Landmark** in your **Inventory** (Ctrl-I), or by looking for the **Landmark** on the **World Map** (Ctrl-M).

◆ *Right-click* on your Avatar and *select* **Profiles** and then the **Picks Tab**.

◆ *Press* the **New** Button and add your own choice of Picture, Title, and Description of your **Pick**.

Profiling Others is Acceptable

Profiling the other Avatars is when you open their **Profile** windows to learn more about them. **Profile** is also an easy way to drop off Inventory items. All you have to do is drag the item onto the **Give Item** area where it prompts you to "**Drop inventory item here.**"

You are also able to use the **Profile Window** to **Pay** (give) them Linden Dollars, send them an **Instant Message**, or invite them to teleport to you. You can also show appreciation by **Rating** them (only positive ratings allowed). To rate, you click on the **Ratings** button and for L$25 you can give a rating. You can only **Rate** that Avatar one time per category. This Linden money does not go to them, it goes to Linden Lab. Your "Given" category in your **Profile Window** is debited with the Rating point you gave.

Profile is also where you can **Mute** particular Avatars if you don't want to hear their **Chat** or receive **Instant Messages** from them. Plus, you already know about the wealth of information you can garner from reading their **Profile** pages.

What Are Groups?

Groups are organizations or communities you can join in Second Life. It keeps people with similar interests in touch. Through the **Group** function you can easily communicate and organize activities. Members can **propose** and **vote** on ideas. It's an excellent way to expand your network within Second Life. Form a **Group** with your friends and join other groups as well.

INFORMATION: GROUPS

To find your listing of **Groups**, *right-click* your Avatar and *select* **Groups** from the pie menu or *left-click* **Edit** from the Menu Bar and select **Groups**.

As you become more familiar with Second Life, **Groups** is a tool that you will want to revisit, especially if you pursue business or land ownership opportunities. Here is some basic information on the special features available to you as a Group member.

Special Titles: Group members and officers are assigned titles. When you click **Groups** on your Avatar pie menu and **activate** and select a **Group** to activate, the Group Title you are assigned will appear over your name. For example: "VIP", "Book Lover", or simply "Member". You can change to the title of any of your groups (or select "no group") at any time by selecting **Groups** on your Avatar pie menu.

INFORMATION: GROUPS (Cont.)

Special Permissions: Group members can be given special permissions and they can vary from one member designation to another. Officers may have more "rights" then a regular "Member". For example, Members can be assigned to be able to modify the builds of the group (when you build with your group tag).

Joint Money Distribution: Groups can be assigned to share in a balance. Any money paid into the group can be assigned to be paid out to group members each day. This is often used when a group owns a business venture jointly.

Joint Land Ownership: Groups can jointly own land, with each member making a contribution to help pay for the land's cost and even contributing their initial 512 sq. meters tier under their premium membership plan. Groups historically have received a 10% bonus allocation to their tier requirement.

Group Member Recognition: Other residents can see what groups you joined by looking on your profile.

JOINING A GROUP

You can join established groups but how you join depends on whether it is designated for Open or Closed enrollment. **Open groups** allow anyone the ability to sign up by clicking the **Join** Button in the **Group** Information window. **Closed Groups** require an invitation first from a **Group Officer** before you are allowed to join.

FINDING GROUPS

There are basically three ways to find **Groups** to join:

PROFILE LIST: Look for the Groups that the other residents have joined. *Right-click* on an Avatar; *select* their **Profile**, and look through their list of **Groups**. If you are interested then *left-click* on the **Group** name and it will open to the **Group Information** page. That page has the **Join** Button available if it is classified as"**Open Group**".

INFORMATION: GROUPS (Cont.)

SEARCH TOOL: Open the **Search Tool** (Ctrl-F); select the **Groups Tab**; use the keyword search approach to find groups that might interest you. This is not a sophisticated search approach. The name will only appear if the search word is the first word in their name.

SL WEBSITE (www.secondlife.com): A more powerful search engine is available on the official SL Website. *Select* "**Community**" from the Menu Bar. The Community page has a Search Box. Use your keyword there to locate a **Group** that uses that word anywhere in their name or description. The search will also produce results for **Events** and **Places**. Once you find **Groups** that pique your interest, look them up in-world, using the **Search Tool** (Ctrl-F) and **Groups Tab**.

PROFILE AND GROUP TIPS AND HINTS:

- You may choose to disclose personal information in your **Profile**, be aware that whatever you write becomes public information.

- The Member Name, Title, and Last Login columns on the Group Member listing can be sorted. If you can view this area for a group, you can see when the individual Members had visited SL last.

- If notices are getting irritating (some groups send a lot of them) you can un-check **Receive Group Notices** under the **General Tab** of the Group Information page for that particular group. This is especially useful if you are getting spammed.

- **Groups** require a minimum of two Members to be called a **Group**; this allows couples and pairs to **Group** easily without involving others. A group can also have more than one Owner.

- You can belong to up to 25 groups at the moment. This is always subject to change. The LL people have already raised it once.

- Groups that own land have a 10% tier bonus.

PROFILE AND GROUP TIPS AND HINTS: (Cont.)

- There is a hierarchy of power in a group based on **Role Assignments**. Any Member in a **Role** with the right **Abilities** can promote and demote other Members from Roles.

- If you have multiple Titles (**Roles**) in a group, you can select from any of their titles by using the **My Active Title** menu that is found on the **General Tab** of the **Group Information** page.

- Anyone can create a new group for L$100. Open the **Group Window** through **Edit** or through your Avatars pie menu and select **Groups**. The **Create** Button allows for easy creation of a **Group**.

- When you **Create** a **Group** you are assigned the **Role** of Founder and also of Owner.

- The **Group Charter** is located on the **General Tab** on the **Group Information** page. This provides a description of what the group is about, a mission statement, or other information of interest.

- Read the **Group Charter**. Also read what rights and responsibilities you have as a member if you join. Be aware that some groups cost to join. Also some groups (especially with group land and business ownership) assign some financial responsibilities to the group members.

- The value of the **Rating** system is yet proven. Linden Lab makes the money but they don't track the ratings at this point. Also friends have been known to give each other ratings regardless. Others have paid people to give then a rate.

- The **Rating** system for **Behavior, Appearance,** and **Building** that Residents use through the **Profile Window** is also known as a **Reputation System**.

Group Quest

In your quest for signing up with a couple of groups, you will noticed that **Groups** center on a particular topic of interest. This gives people a common ground for discussion and is an easy way to meet people through common interest. Some of the SL Groups have formed their own websites. **Groups** are also used as the corporation equivalent in Second Life. The **Group** in this case may provide a service, make and sell a product, rent or manage property, etc.

Some residents set up **Groups** to re-enact some specific world or place in time. Using land they may recreate this world and the participants are required to dress, act, and speak according to the time period. These role-play worlds extend even beyond creating from literature, history, or specific geography. Geography examples include replicating Las Vegas, New York, or Paris; or replicating Historical events like WWII, or ancient worlds like medieval Japan, or ancient Rome in a Region. However, residents are always free to move in and out of these worlds as they see fit. Land ownership and property rights, however, often dictate with the property owner choosing to expel residents who don't abide by the defined property regulations or the community standard of acceptance.

There are also areas that re-create worlds from literature or specific geography. Some of the **Groups** (often referred to as subcultures) in Second Life evolve around interests and events. These will include activities related to sports, arts, religion, charity, support groups, commerce, culture, education, warring, games, contests, nightlife, entertainment, and pageants. If there is an interest, then someone, somewhere in Second Life is bound to create or re-create it. This is the uniqueness of Second Life and what makes it the growing phenomena that it is.

CHAPTER 15:
FRIENDSHIP RINGS
Be True To Thyself

Let Me Call You Sweetheart

Friends hold a special standing in Second Life. There is a **Friends** button (Ctrl-Shift-F) dedicated to assisting with the management of your network. Easily add Friends, communicate, track and even share rights to modify objects and items. Once you get the hang of the Friends tool, you will see how powerful it really is.

INFORMATION: FRIENDS (Ctrl-Shift-F)

Select more than one friend on your list by using Ctrl-*select* or Shift-*select* functions.

PERMISSIONS WITH FRIENDS

For each Friend, or Group of Friends, selected you can choose to allow them the following privileges (displayed by an icon) by checking the corresponding box:

Can see my online status: Friends on your list are notified when you enter SL. They are only notified if they are already in-world.

Can see me on the map: Allow your friends to track you on the World Map. They can then look up your location.

INFORMATION: FRIENDS (Cont.)

Can modify my objects: Tick this and you allow your Friends to have **Full Permission** to work with your items. Then you don't need to reset permissions and physically transfer items to them.

BUTTON FUNCTIONS:

Instant Message (IM): Start a private text conversation with one or more Friends.

Profile: Select and open a Profile Window on a Friend.

Pay: Transfer Linden Dollars to a Friend.

Add: Invite someone to your Friend's list.

Remove: Remove someone from your list.

Tell One and All

You know you can text message with one person in IM, but you can also text message with a lot of people all at once. Along with friends, your **Instant Message** (Ctrl-T) will also show any Groups you are a member of at the top of the **New IM** Tab.

Opening the text box by *double-clicking* the **Group** name will message everyone who is online, and in that group, all at the same time. Then any or all of them can respond at once.

Everyone in the group then is party to the conversation. It's a great tool, but irritating when people use Group messaging for private conversations meant for only a few. That's often when the Mute function is invoked by the members. That's also when members will remind people to take their conversation offline.

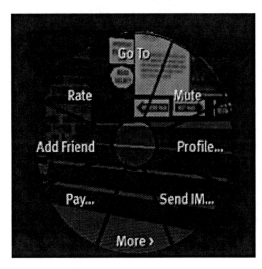

FRIENDSHIP TIPS AND HINTS:

- To give something to someone nearby just *drag* the item from **Inventory** and *drop* it onto the other resident's Avatar.

- To simply give another Resident your Calling Card without adding them as a friend, *right-click* on their Avatar, click on more, then select **Give Card**.

- If you're near them, just right-click their Avatar in-world and *select* **Add Friend**.

- If you're not near them, or if they're offline, *click* the **Friends** button at the bottom of the screen to bring up your friend list. Then *click* the **Add...** button. That brings up a search dialog where you can find someone by name to offer them friendship.

- You can give someone an item by dragging the item directly onto their Calling Card. Alternatively, open their Calling Card, and *drop* the item onto their **Profile**.

- If you want to give an item without using the Calling Card, Open **Search** (Ctrl-F), and search for the person under the **People Tab**. *Click* their name see their **Profile**, and *drop* the item onto their **Profile**. If an item is marked as **No Copy**, you will transfer then the item and lose the ownership if the other person accepts the transfer.

- If an item is marked as **No Transfer**, you will be unable to give the item to another Avatar.

- Your Calling Card Inventory is not automatically reflected in your **Friends Window**. When you add someone as a friend and it is accepted, their name automatically lists on the Friends List and a Calling Card is added to **Inventory**.

- When you join or create a Second Life **Group**, the **IM** window will display a listing for your groups. You can *double-click* the **Group** name to start an **IM** session with all online members of the **Group** at once.

- You can also create other **IM** groups of residents that you want to communicate with regularly by creating a "Calling Card" folder for a group of people.

FRIENDSHIP TIPS AND HINTS: (Cont.)

- If you keep getting these offline emails through Calling Card messaging, you can *delete* the Calling Card for that individual and your card will automatically delete from their folder. Friendship is mutual.

- You can always track the online status of people using the **Search** (Ctrl-F) function without having it report directly to you when they are online or not.

- Residents who refer their friends are presently receiving a single lump sum payment of L$2000 for each friend who signs up for a Premium Ac count.

- You can refer as many friends as you like to Second Life and the same bonus will apply to all of them as long as they sign up. (There used to be a limit of 5).

- The **People Tab** is where you can search for other Residents, and Linden staff. Only the current and active accounts are listed.

Calling All Cards

The Calling Card is an **Inventory Only Item**. That means it cannot be manipulated outside of the Inventory environment. Calling Cards are also called the shortcut to another resident's profile. Just *double left-click* on a Calling Card and that Resident's **Profile Window** opens.

Calling Cards are different from the action of inviting **Friendship**. With Calling Cards you can give another resident a calling card without receiving one in return. In friendship it has to be a mutual exchange. Also, calling cards do not track through the Friends feature on the **World Map** (Ctrl-M) unless they are also a friend.

Calling Cards are great for remembering people you met. They can easily be sorted into file folders. This is similar to real life use of the Business Card. In early SL these Calling Cards were counted and a bonus was awarded to the residents who held the most. The original Calling Cards influenced the development of the Rating System (referred to also as a Reputation System).

Another use of Calling Cards is to sort them for Conference Calling or "Group Talk". **Create a Folder** in your **Inventory** (Ctrl-I) and *drag* in the Calling Cards of the people you want in a "Group Talk" session. Then *right-click* that folder within your **Inventory** and choose **Instant Message All Users** to send them all a message. Alternatively, you can choose **Instant Message Online Users**. This will only send the "Group Talk" to those currently in Second Life. So don't forget to collect Calling Cards by trading them, or by offering **Friendship** to the people you know or want to keep in touch with. This is the easiest way to stay connected.

EXERCISE 15: SET UP GROUP TALK

OFFER FRIENDSHIP

The only way to get comfortable is to just jump right in and be friendly. Try to find a way today to use all three approaches to extending Friendship.

♦ Offer Friendship to by *right-clicking* on an Avatar and *selecting* **Add Friend**

♦ Give someone a Calling Card without adding them as a **Friend**. *Right-click* on their Avatar, *select* **More**, and *select* **Give Card**.

♦ Offer Friendship to an Avatar by looking up their name in the **People Tab** in **Search** (Ctrl-F) and offer them Friendship through their **Profile**.

♦ *Left-click* Friends (Ctrl-Shift-F) and search for a name of someone you know or met, and select **Add**.

♦ When your Friendship has been received and accepted, then click on the **Friends** Button (Ctrl-Shift-F) and set your permissions for them.

CREATE A "GROUP TALK" FOLDER:

♦ Open your **Inventory** (Ctrl-I), and **Create** a **New folder** within the **Calling Cards** folder. Name that folder something that you recognize about a Group of friends (such as "Frat Brothers", "Best Friends", or "Techies").

♦ Drag the Calling Cards of the **Friends** you want in that new folder. If you *right-click* a Calling Card and *select* **Copy** (Ctrl-C), then *right-click* the folder and *select* **Paste** (Ctrl-V), then you can place the same person in multiple folders.

♦ Now you can start an **IM** session with all the **Friends** in that folder. *Right-click* that folder select either **Instant Message Online Users** or **Instant Message All Users**.

♦ **Instant Message Online Users** includes only those people in the folder who are presently online.

♦ **Instant Message All Users** sends the message to everyone in the folder. Offline residents will receive the message upon logging into Second Life. Those messages will be delayed.

IMPORTANT: The Friends who have their IM sent to their email (by selection in their preferences) will receive a single email for every line of an **Instant Message All Users** conversation. This can result in overload and is a nuisance to the receiver. So choose to use this feature sparingly.

```
SHORTCUT COMMANDS:

Friends*              Ctrl-Shift-F
IM                    Ctrl-T
Select All            Ctrl-A
Copy                  Ctrl-C
Paste                 Ctrl-V

*toggles on/off
```

Handshake or a Kiss

Interaction between residents is largely informal. Handshakes are uncommon but hugs and kisses abound. As far as the more affectionate acts of sex or other related acts, it's not often publicly witnessed due to the stringent TOS/CS (Terms of Service/Community Standards) rules. Though pretty much everything is available and some unique poses are known to exist.

These acts are typically taken to the more private skyboxes, restricted access properties, or membership only clubs. Residents use these alternative options for privacy, whether it be sexual acts or just the typically want of being alone without disturbance. It is easy for the public to see what you are doing because, through the view function (Ctrl-Alt or Alt-*move mouse*), it is easy to pan through walls and doors. As a result, people who want privacy will usually try to be discreet.

Sky Boxes are often found at very high altitudes and are out of sight to most residents. To reach them, when they are at great heights, often requires either a direct teleport that is structured by the owner, or you have to ride an object up to get there. These Sky Boxes may also be accompanied by security "scripts" that can eject (from the land) or send home the unwanted peeping toms and intruders. So when you are walking or flying around Second Life, look around, look up, and you shall find more than what you originally thought was there.

CHAPTER 16:
PHONE HOME
Mapping It Out

Map and Find It!

Maps are useful for navigating around Second Life and finding locations, people, and activities of interest. There are two types of Maps, the **Mini-Map** (Ctrl-Shift-M) and **World Map** (Ctrl-M). These two maps are integrated, and upon directly opening them, they display your Avatar's location. The Mini-Map is used for navigation and tracking. This map displays the immediate vicinity around your location upon opening. The Yellow dot is you and the white triangle is your "field of vision" showing the direction you are facing. Any objects that you own appear on the mini-map in light blue. This feature can be useful in identifying the location of your objects. Each green dot on both maps is another resident. On the mini-map groups of people appear in clusters. Click on the mini-map and the World Map opens.

Open the World Map and again you appear in the center as a yellow circle. Again a white triangle appears showing the direction you are facing. This map shows a lot more detail. In the World Map groups of people appear stacked. The World Map can also be opened through **Search**, **SLURLs**, and **Landmarks**.

INFORMATION: MINI MAP (Ctrl-Shift-M)

MINI-MAP

This is a small map that can be useful to navigate around Second Life. *Select* **View** from the Menu Bar and select **Mini-Map** (Ctrl-Shift-M). The **Mini-Map** appears in the right hand top corner but like all of the Windows in Second Life, you can *left-click*, *hold*, and *drag* it around.

Yellow Dot: This represents you as your reference point. You can see where you are located.

Cone of Light: Emanates from the **Yellow Dot** and shows which direction you're facing.

INFORMATION: MINI MAP (Ctrl-Shift-M) (Cont.)

Green Dots: These are all the other Avatars around you. If the **Green Dot** is **round**, then that Avatar is at about the same height as you. If the **Green Dot** looks like a "T", then the Avatar is above you in height. They may be flying, or in a very high building. If the "T" appears **upside down**, then the Avatar is somewhere below you.

Compass: North (N) on the map is in a bluer shade than the other directions. This is done to help you orient yourself. If you move your Avatar in circles you will see that the **Mini-Map** will track with you.

Geographic Features: Land Type is represented in color. Grass is green, snow is white, and water is blue.

Dark Gray Blocks: These represent Objects that are owned by others. In a region with lots of buildings, you will see lots of dark gray blocks.

Cyan Blocks: This color shows which Objects you own in the area. This can be useful for finding lost objects.

Fuchsia Blocks: These Objects are owned by a group of which you are a member. For an object to be group-owned it must be set to "**Share with group**" and you need to activate and wear your group name in order for your group-ownership to be recognized.

Regions: The Regions are defined by squares. The region you are in will be lighter than adjacent ones. You can see this more clearly by *click dragging* on the orange triangle in the lower right corner of the **Mini-Map** which will resize it.

Dark Gray Areas: This is area beyond the borders of the World so you can't go there.

Left-clicking **on the Mini-Map:** This action opens the larger **World Map.** The **World Map** shows more detail about your Region and the Regions around you.

Right-clicking **on the Mini-Map:** Lets you change the zoom level and "Stop Tracking". Tracking is caused by clicking the map or by using the Search function. When you are tracking you see a red beacon and an arrow pointing to a destination.

Home Sweet "Home"

Everyone needs to have a place where they feel they belong. A place where you can start your day and a place you find is your haven. One way to find a home is to own land. Others decide to be renters, instead. Another approach is to belong to a group that owns land. With a group title you can then set the location in the **World** in the Menu Bar and select **Set Home to Here**. This way, if you wander off and end up in a damage-enabled area and are killed; death means an instant teleport back to your home location. Nothing bad happens, you just go home. "Home is where the heart is" and it's taken quite literally. Your health is restored there. If you don't have a location to call your own, the only home alternative is a Mainland InfoHub. Either way, you need to search for a place to call **Home**.

EXERCISE 16: ESTABLISH YOURSELF

ESTABLISH YOUR "HOME"

You will feel less like a Newbie if you can establish a Home. Your options are to own or rent. In the next Chapter we address the topic of Land ownership.

- ◆ Go to your Land, rental space, or Mainland InfoHub (noted by a blue i Icon on the World Map).

- ◆ *Left-click* **World** in the Menu Bar and select **Set Home to Here**.

- ◆ Open the **World Map** and find the blue house icon which is now your new Home.

ESTABLISH A LANDMARK

In Chapter 5 you searched Sandbox space for building. When you were there, you should have created a Landmark so it is easy to return after your explorations. If you didn't, this is a good time to set one up. Also, in the Appendix is a suggested list of places to Explore.

- ◆ Go to the Appendix and find the **SL Explore Recommendations** and pick out a few places that sound interesting. Teleport to them through the **World Map**.

- ◆ Once there, explore a little. If it is a place you find interesting, go ahead and set a Landmark by *left-clicking* **World** on your Menu Bar, *select* **Create Landmark Here**.

- ◆ If you like the location, take a couple of **Snapshots** (Ctrl-Shift-S) and save them to your hard drive in a **SL Explore Tour** folder. Label the first photo for the file "Explore 1" (Then next time you are in-world, start that SL photo series as "Explore 2". The individual photos will automatically be assigned as _001, _002, etc.)

- ◆ The **Landmark** Window gives you the choice to "**Teleport**" or "**Show on Map**". Since you want neither right now, just close the window by *left-clicking* the "**X**" in the right hand corner (Ctrl-W).

- ◆ Open your **Inventory** (Ctrl-I) and find your Landmark filed under the **Landmarks** folder. Notice it has defaulted to the location title.

♦ *Right-click* that Landmark file and select **Rename** from the Context Menu. If this is your Sandbox Name it "My Sandbox." If it is an SL Explore Location, give it a name you will re-member.

SET UP A TOUR PACKAGE

You should start collecting Landmarks from favorite places. To keep them organized you can set them up into a Folder for easy finding.

♦ Select the **Landmarks** folder; right-click on it and select **New Folder** from the Context Menu.

♦ Select **New Folder**; *right-click* and select **Rename**. Label it "SL Explore Landmarks"

♦ Now *left-click drag* the Landmark files into that folder. See how many of the SL Explore Tour recommendations you can establish as Landmarks.

♦ *Select* one of the Landmarks in your **SL Explore Landmarks** folder. *Right-click*, select **Prop-erties**. Notice that the Default permission settings allow the next owner full rights to **Copy**, **Modify**, and **Transfer**. Leave the default set as is.

♦ Now package your tour. **Create** a Cube (Ctrl-4) and *drag* the **SL Explore Landmarks** folder into the Cube. Set the **Permissions** on the cube to allow the next owner to **Copy** and **Trans-fer** only.

♦ To make the Tour Package look interesting, wrap the Cube with Snapshots by using Upload Textures (Ctrl-U) to add your favorite SL Explore Landmarks snapshots to your **Inventory** from your hard drive. There are 6 faces to your Cube. Place a different Snapshot (or Texture) on each face (see Chapter 10 for details).

Now that your Tour is packaged, you can give them as gifts to friends. Add a note card so they have in-formation about how to take the Tour.

SET UP A TOUR ITINERARY

A Tour Itinerary is similar to a Tour Package except that instead of Boxing the Tours, you add the Tours to a Note. This gives you greater flexibility since you can write a description of the location and even add a picture or two with the Landmark.

♦ **Create the New Note** in **Inventory** (Ctrl-I); *left-click* **Create,** *select* **New Note** The New Note file can be found in your **Notecards** folder and should open upon creation. *Right-click* the file and rename it "SL Explore Itinerary" and the opened note's name will automatically change.

♦ If the note didn't open, *Double Left-click* the **SL Explore Itinerary note** and it will open or *right-click* the note and *select* **Open**. Type in a Description: "Fun and Interesting Tours in SL".

♦ Now type up a short Introduction. Then referencing your **Landmarks**, type the title of the first location onto your note, provide a short description, and then *drag* onto the note (from your Inventory file) the Landmark that corresponds to it. If you have a picture of the location, drag that onto the notecard as well. See what happens? This makes it easy for someone to follow your tour in the order you define on the note.

♦ When you are done, press **Save**, and it will return to **Inventory**.

♦ If you don't want the next owner to **Modify** the itinerary, then *right-click* the file and change the **Properties**. Now to give the Itinerary as a gift it doesn't need to be "Unboxed" you can simply drop it onto someone's **Profile** and they have it all intact to follow.

INFORMATION: WORLD MAP (Ctrl-M)

MARKERS

- **You (Yellow Circle):** The reference point for where you are standing.

- **Your Home (Blue House):** Location where you set your "Home".

- **Classifieds (Green Hand):** Locations that have a Classified Listing.

- **Residents (Green Dots):** Other Avatars in the World.

- **InfoHub (Blue I Circle):** Information designed Hub.

- **TeleHub (Blue/Yellow Cross)**: Established Teleport location for the Region

- **Land for Sale (Yellow):** Border designation for Land Listed for Sale.

- **Price Listing for Land (Dollar Tag):** Sell Price set by owner. Select for description, size, and price.

- **Popular Places (Yellow Thumbs):** Achieved the Top 20 List for Traffic in the last 24 hour period.

- **Events (Pink Stars):** Mouse Over to read PG event listed on Search.

- **Mature Events (Blue Star "M"):** Mouse Over to read Mature event listed on Search.

- **Auction (Blue/Purple):** Land on the Auction Block found in Search.

TABS:
You can choose from 2 types of views on the **World Map**

Objects: Reflects Objects built and overlaying the Ground

Terrain: Only displays the view of the actual ground and water format.

INFORMATION: WORLD MAP (Ctrl-M) (Cont.)

TABS:

You can choose from 2 types of views on the **World Map**

Objects: Reflects Objects built and overlaying the Ground

Terrain: Only displays the view of the actual ground and water format.

OPTIONS:

Home (Go Home): This button transports you immediately to your designated home location.

Teleport: Allows you to click on a location and be transported directly there.

Friends: This drop down menu brings up the names of all of your friends that are online so that you can click on their name and it will show their location. You can then choose to teleport directly to them.

Find Region: You can fill in the name of a region and the actual coordinates of a location. It will be located on the map indicated by a red hollow circle. Then you can teleport there.

Landmarks: This is a list of the locations you have stored in your Landmarks folder in Inventory. You can either double left-click the landmark in the folder or use the drop down list and see the location in the map view.

Show Destination: Where you are going (per your selection) is displayed on the map with a red circle on the map and a red marker arrow will appear near your Avatar with the distance in-world from your location. If you turn in the direction of the arrow you will see a red light beam in the distance marking the location. You can fly toward that beam and see the listed meter distance decrease as you get closer to your destination.

Show My Location: which is where you presently are located. You can toggle this button with **Show Destination.** This toggle is useful when flying across Regions and when you are searching for a specific coordinate set.

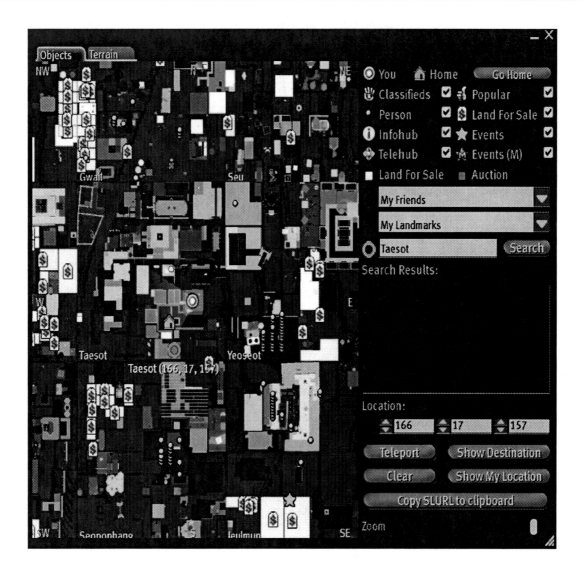

MAP TIPS AND HINTS:

- If a region is Offline it will appear red. It indicates there is a problem and you can't go there. You can keep an eye on it through the **World Map** (Ctrtl-M). if it seems to be Offline too long, you can also inquiry about it through the **Help Request** in the **Help on your** Menu Bar

- The destination you select on the **World Map** will be marked with a red arrow and a red pillar of light when you teleport to it if you can't teleport directly onto the coordinates. Simply fly or walk toward the red pillar of light then to get there.

- Objects will show up on the world Map, but they have to be lower than 400 meters.

MAP TIPS AND HINTS:

- Landmarks come in two different colors. Bright red landmarks are ones you've already used and teleported to. The color will then change when you open a new session. The more faded mauve landmarks are ones you haven't been to yet.

- The Mini-map displays the sim immediately surrounding your Avatar. It shows the layout of the sim including buildings and terrain. The dot in the middle represents you, and the white cone is your field of vision. The Mini-map rotates as you turn, making it easy to keep to a compass heading if you choose to.

- The Mini-Map displays all the objects you own in light blue.

- The default permission settings for Landmarks allow the next owner full rights to Copy, Modify, and Transfer.

- The World Map is also on the web on the Second Life website (http://secondlife.com/) or on SLURL (http://slurl.com/).

- A home location is set from the **World** menu, but will works only if you are over land you own or have permission rights to set a landmark.

- A blue house icon on the World map that shows you where your home is located.

SLURLing Your Words?

A SLURL (Second Life URL) provides a convenient bridge between two worlds. They connect between what you see and read in the real world with where you need to go for the experience in Second Life. This is done through a simple teleport link. The advantage of using a SLURL format outside of SL is that the website (www.slurl.com) makes it easy for a new participant who is interested to sign up for SL. This more sophisticated SLURL maker also allows easy formatting of the billboard offered on the map. You can add your own title, text, a picture, or even a website window. This is an intriguing way for you to provide a glimpse to the other party of what to expect at the other end of the teleport.

Residents easily communicate to other residents by offering SLURLs through email, blogs, and websites. Clicking on a SLURL link opens the SL map. From the map you can choose to teleport (which will open an SL session), and directly populate the coordinates into your World Map. It's the easiest way to get people to a designated location.

TIME TO SLURL IT UP

MAKE A SIMPLE SLURL

SLURL your Sandbox location. Open the **World Map** and *click* on **Show my location**; click **Copy Slurl to Clipboard**. Then paste (Ctrl-V) the SLURL onto a Notepad, Word Document, or anything that accepts text. It should look something like this:

http://slurl.com/secondlife/Taesot/159/56/24

Notice that the SLURL simply adds Region and the X, Y, and Z coordinates of your location. Look at the top of your Menu Bar in Second Life. Notice the same coordinates appear there. Now *Ctrl-click* on the SLURL address and the SLURL Website opens. The World Map will appear with the location your standing at with a marker pointing to it. Be patient, it may take awhile for your browser to respond.

SLURL WITH A PICTURE

Adding a picture to replace the Second Life box on the SLURL is easy. Using your Internet Browser, go to **www.slurl.com**. *Click* on **Build your own Slurls.** On the form below Location Data, put in your Region's name, and the 3 coordinates.

Skip over Window Image Size. In the **Window Title** space type in: "My Sandbox". Then upload one of your self-portrait snapshots from your hard drive onto a free photo sharing website like Photo-bucket (**www.photobucket.com**) or Snapzilla (**www.slpics.com**).

Follow their Upload instructions, then copy the URL for the photo; paste it onto the SLURL form **Window Image** space. Add a **Window Message** also.

Press Generate Slurl. Now the SLURL appears at the bottom of the page. Press **Go** and take a look at your SLURL.

TIME TO SLURL IT UP (Cont.)

SLURL WITH A WEBSITE LINK

Using the same SLURL form above, this time add a web address where it says Insert IFRAME. That is any web address you want to window in. Just pick any web address from the Internet, but make sure you copy the address as it reads in your Internet Browser window. Then *press* **Generate Slurl**, and the "**Go**" button to view.

If it looks good, then you just copy the SLURL address to share in emails, Blogs, Websites, MySpace, and pretty much anywhere.

SLURL TIPS AND HINTS:

- To activate the button that creates SLURLs in the World Map, just choose a **Friend**, **Landmark**, or search for a Region. When the coordinates on the World Map populate, you are able to create the SLURL through the Map function "Copy Slurl to Clipboard."

- Once the SLURL is on the clipboard, you can open your web browser and paste it into the address bar and press enter to see what it does (it may take awhile, please be patient).

- You can paste a SLURL into anything that accepts text like a MySpace page, a Blog page, in an email, or just on a blank Word page. To activate the SLURL requires only a *Ctrl-click*.

- You can teleport your Avatar directly to a location using the **Teleport** button on the SLURL map.

- SLURLs are used on fan sites, advertising products for sale, blog articles, websites, etc.

SLURL TIPS AND HINTS: (Cont.)

- Social websites like Snapzilla and SLBuzz even take the snapshots you email out of Second Life and post them on the web with SLURLS. If you want, they even have cross-posting options to popular photo-sharing website Flickr, spreading your SLURLs further in the process.

- Please note that precision of teleporting to a given location depends on how the owner set the land option. The owner may have chosen to override the teleport coordinates by having all teleports directed to a particular landing point. This is often done in Malls so store owners cannot direct traffic solely to their store, but instead through the landing point so the whole mall gains the exposure.

- Both Landmarks and SLURLs have the same purpose. They both are designed to help you pinpoint and get to a particular destination quickly.

- However: Landmarks are an item type in your Inventory, so they're not usable outside of Second Life. If you want to share a specific location with friends on the web, you'll need to use a SLURL.

- SLURLs are better than just using a www.secondlife.com prefix reference because the SLURL will at least inform someone first about what they're getting into, offers added customization, and provides a link to join Second Life.

- A great companion for SLURLs (since they tend to be lengthy) is TinyURL. Just like the name says, it creates an alias (redirect) which leads to your SLURL.

- Linden Lab often uses what is called a TinyURL Since long URLs are more prone to break due to various causes like human error (not copied and pasted correctly) or bugs (email client's line breaks chop it in half), the TinyURL reformats the SLURL to make it brief. SLURLs can be converted to TinyURLs (www.TinyUrl.com).

SL Space is Universal

In Second Life there's something new (and different) around every corner. In previous chapters we recommended Search sites and encouraged exploration. Out of curiosity you probably have already found casinos, dance clubs, amusement parks, theme regions, shopping malls, space stations, vampire castles, dance clubs, and movie theatres.

Make sure you explore the Appendix Website Resources at the back of this book, to experience the merging of Second Life with the real world through the use of SLURLS, websites, news resources, blogs, and product exchanges.

Talking with the other residents you have met, the world as you know it probably just got a whole lot bigger. SL has probably introduced you to people from all over the country as well

from all over the world. You should be trading Calling Cards, joining Groups, and expanding your network of Friends.

You are almost at the end of this book, and now should realize how far you have come in your knowledge of SL. Yet there is always more to learn and do. Don't worry, no one ever knows it all or does it all, just enjoy the journey.

CHAPTER 17:
ONE IF BY LAND
Two If By Sea

To Buy or Not to Buy

Sooner or later the SL residents who make a commitment to this new world decide they want land. What motivates this desire will vary. Sometimes a resident just wants a home. Others decide they want a place to leave their builds, entertain their friends, set up a business, or just feel part of a community. There are two options available for your own personal space. You can basically choose to own or rent. There are very important differences between these two, which we will explain in this chapter.

Owning It

This is very similar to owning real estate in the real world. You buy land, you pay property tax (called a monthly tier), and you can benefit from land value appreciating. You also have the right to sell it. Sound familiar? If you talk to the established residents, most will agree that it is the recommended route even though it is more expensive. Land ownership offers greater security and fewer restrictions.

To own land you have to upgrade first to a premium account. This means that there is a monthly membership fee. However, the membership does give you a sign on bonus and a weekly stipend which makes it almost feel like its paying for itself; although, the stipends paid under the membership program have been decreasing as the volume of residents grows. You can reduce your membership cost by paying for a year at a time. That is definitely well worth it if you are making a long-term commitment.

INFORMATION: PREMIUM MEMBERSHIP UPGRADE

You can only purchase land if you hold a Premium Membership in Second Life. At the time of this printing, the Premium Membership cost can be reduced by paying quarterly or yearly. It also provides a Sign on Bonus, Monthly Stipend, and no tier fee for the first 512 sq meters of land that you own. Though the price and value of membership keeps changing, it still seems to be a good deal when added up. However, like every good deal, there is still a payout. You need to weigh your level of commitment and evaluate your purpose for pursuing land ownership.

INFORMATION: PREMIUM MEMBERSHIP UPGRADE (Cont.)

Don't worry if you have a free account (Basic Membership) right now. You can always upgrade at anytime to a Premium Membership and enjoy these benefits. Check the Second Life website for the going fees and associated benefit amounts.

When you are ready to upgrade; just log into your account on the Second Life website (www.secondlife.com) using your Avatar name and password. In the upper right hand corner of your screen, click **My Account**, Find the link titled **Upgrade/Downgrade Account** and select a Premium Option Account and Payment Method that works for you.

EXERCISE 17: LANDING IT

LAYOUT THE METERS

♦ Measure out 512 sq. meters to get a good idea of the size relative to your Avatar. Find your Sandbox again. This time build a 512 sq. meter platform in the sky. That means, if a flattened Prim is 10m x 10m or 100 sq. meters, then approximately 5 flattened Prims side by side would be 500 sq. meters.

♦ Create a Cube (Ctrl-4) in the air (high enough to be out of everyone's way so fly up a bit). Now stretch and flatten that Cube to be (Size: X=10.0m, Y=10.0m, Z=0.010m). Stand on it.

♦ Now in Edit mode, Copy by Shift left-click drag on either the green or red arrow. Set the X position for that Cube to be 10.0m more than the position of X the first cube. (For example, if X_1-Position =128.00 then X_2-Position = 138.00 and X_3-Position = 148.00)

♦ Copy until you have a total of 5 flat squares touching.

♦ Rearrange these squares to form a couple different property shapes, but the size now of your platform consisting of 5 fully stretched and flattened Cubes is basically the size of your 512 sq. meters of land that does not require a tier fee.

SEARCH LAND PARCELS
Window shop and visit 512 sq. meter parcels in the market.

◆ Open up **Search** (Ctrl-F); select the **Land Sales** Tab. Enter 512 sq. meters in the space for parcel size and press the Search button.

◆ Scroll down and select a 512 sq. meter parcel that looks reasonable and Teleport to it (regardless of price, location, or type of land). We are just looking at sizing.

◆ Once on the land, *right-click* the ground and select **About Land**. The plot size will outline in red. This gives you an idea of size.

◆ You can do this a couple of different times. Also note the listing in the **Search** window when you select it. Start getting familiar with the listings, the price, covenants, and whether it is for sale or rent.

LOOK AT THE WORLD MAP
Compare different plot sizes.

◆ Now open the **World Map** (Ctrl-M), and check the box that says **Land for Sale** (has a $ icon in front of it). The land parcels for sale now appear in yellow.

◆ Zoom in and out of the **World Map** by *left-clicking* the map and *scrolling* your mouse wheel. See all the land parcels for sale?

◆ *Click* on some of the $ icons. A description of the land, size, and price will appear. Look around. Find a couple of plots to visit. Visit land that is 512 sq meters, 1,024 sq. meters, 1,536 sq. meters and a couple of larger plots.

◆ Teleport to the land plots by *double-clicking* the parcel on the map and teleporting there.

◆ *Right-click* the ground and select **About Land** (or left-click **World** on the top menu bar and select **About Land**). Walk around, how does the space feel to you?

◆ Pay attention to the price on the 512 sq. meter plots for sale. This gives you an idea of the current market price of ownership for the smallest plot. This you can compare to the same size plots for rent.

Too Tight for Comfort?

For a lot of people 512 sq meters is a tight space. But then, that really depends on what you are going to do with it, and where it is located. Placing a store, casino, or a house border to border with neighboring buildings towering right up against your property line, may not be the most attractive location. The other question to ask yourself "Is it sufficient for your purpose?" Also pay attention to the amount of Prims allowed on the land. In **Chapter 9** we addressed the formula for determining maximum Prim counts per parcel of land.

When you open the **About Land** window the amount of Prims allowed on the parcel is listed under the Objects Tab or do the math. A 512 sq. meter plot allows usually 117 Prims (.229 x 512 sq. m = 117). Some parcels may allow less or more for various reasons, but typically it will be around 117 Prims. Sound like a lot?

COUNTING PRIMS

The only way you are going to get a feel for square meter plots and the Prim allotment is to go window shopping. In the last exercise you measured and researched lots. Now let's count Prims for a Home.

HOME COUNT

Search (Ctrl-F) using the keywords "prefab houses" or "houses," use the **All Tab**. *Select* a result that looks promising and teleport there. With pencil in hand, look around and see what you can find that will fit on a 512 sq. meter lot. *Right-click* the house and *select* **Edit** to find the Prim count. The sales literature may also have the Prim count posted.

Remember that you will want some space for entry or a yard (this is especially important if your neighbors erect tall buildings around you or they own large plots and block you in with a wall. Though remember you can float your house but a platform adds to your Prim count.

Once you have the Prim count written down for several houses that fit your lot size, move on to find furnishings. **Search** (Ctrl-F) using the keyword "Furniture", and go shopping with pencil and paper again in hand. Select various items you might be interested in and note the amount of Prims. You can start noting prices as well so you have an idea of costs. We will address jobs a bit later on and other ways to make money will be a subject for another book.

When you are done furnishing your dream house, add up the Prims, and what is your total? Depending on what you plan to do with the parcel will dictate whether 512 sq. meters and 117 Prims is right for you. Most find it small, but it is a starting point.

INFORMATION: PURCHASING LAND

BUYING LAND

The available land that is for sale can be viewed through the **Search** (Ctrl-F) function. The search results sort in alphabetical order and also by land size, and price. Another approach is to use the **World Map** and look at the plots for sale by zooming in and out of Regions. This sometimes is easier to window shop since you can get a general idea of what is built around the plots and gain a better perspective when comparing prices and location.

Once you find a plot you are interested in, teleport to it, and check the **Property Borders** (P). Then *right-click* the Land and select **About Land** to read the tabs to know what you are buying. **Landmark** it and file them into an **Inventory** folder for later reference.

When you are ready to Buy a plot, teleport to it, *right-click* the Land and *select* **Buy Land**; or right click the land, select **About Land** and *select* the **Buy Land** button on the **General Tab**. Make sure you have enough money in your account to make the purchase. Remember you have to hold a premium membership to buy land. If the land is more than 512 sq. meters, then you will also be responsible for the monthly tier fee.

TIER FEES

Also referred to as a monthly use fee. The fees are charged for parcels AFTER the first 512 sq. meters. This chart represents the additional land purchased and the associated monthly fee. These fees are subject to change so check the Second Life website the latest information. Monthly fees are required to be paid in US dollars.

PLOT SIZE	MONTHLY FEE
512 sq m	US$5
1,024 sq m	US$8
2,048 sq m	US$15
4,096 sq m	US$25
8,192 sq m	US$40
16,384 sq m	US$75
32,768 sq m	US$125
65,536 sq m	US$195

Know Thyself, and Thy Land

Land can be edited (or "terraformed") in many ways: flattened, smoothed, raised, roughened, etc. So if it isn't perfect for you, you can change it. Read the covenants and restrictions to make sure you can change it the way you plan—before you buy it. For example a residential area may be zoned and doesn't allow for a business. A snow region can't have grass. Or the height of your ground cannot exceed a certain height.

LAND TIPS AND HINTS:

- Tier free Land is only 512 square meters. Even though it is land to buy and there is no Tier fee, it really isn't much land at all.

- Always shop around before you make that buy decision for property. An emotional or impulsive buy always ends off costing more.

- The same questions need to be asked in SL that you ask yourself when you buy property in RL. What kind of view will you have? What are the neighbors like? Is it conveniently located for you? Do you like the geography? Is it close to your friends? Is it close to where you like to hang out?

- Other questions that become important have to do with traffic causing lag. Does the sim host many events? Is there continuously 30-40 people stacked in a single location (like a club or casino)? This might look good for a business, but if the casino has campers that sit for hours and the sim is often full, your business won't grow.

- You can buy land directly from Linden Labs through the land auctions. You can buy land for Linden Dollars (L$) or for US dollars.

- Sort the land listings by sale price to be able to compare the L$/meter to be an informed consumer.

- The price listed is not fixed. The land owner can set the price to whatever they want. You can approach (Instant Message) the owner and see if you can negotiate a lower price. When land owners have tier fees and their property is not selling, often you can negotiate a lower price.

- Talk with the other residents and your friends, often they will hear or see a good land deal.

LAND TIPS AND HINTS (Cont.)

- Remember that Builds are easily changed so land around you can be redeveloped overnight. Next door may be a private residence or junk yard one day and a skyscraper or casino the next.

- Rule of thumb, it you don't like what's there today, WAIT, it might change to something new in a couple days.

- Land Sales are always directly between the buyer and the seller. This ensures that, at the moment of the transaction, the seller is in fact authorized to sell the property and the buyer, in fact has the money to buy the property. There is never a question of title in SL, all plots and parcels are clearly marked.

- Sale prices on land vary greatly even within the same region. So shop around.

- Most of all, before you buy land, make sure you're familiar with how Second Life bills for land. Read up on the Land FAQ on the Second Life website before making a purchase.

- The Land Sales tab in Search also shows land other residents have for sale. While the prices on these parcels are generally higher, there are a lot more of them available. Larger size parcels are also frequently available and don't assume bigger is always better or cheaper $L/meter.

- Make sure you read the About Land to confirm the type of transaction. Rentals, Co-Ops and other creative forms of Land sharing are offered through Land for Sale ads.

- Second Life also has Land Auctions for selling land. Find it in the Land for Sale listings. In the World Map this land appears to be bluish purple in color. Auctions have a set closing time, and the land goes to the highest bidder. Auction parcels sell for Linden Dollars (L$) as well as US dollars (USD$).

Landing It

Owning land in Second Life allows you greater flexibility to build, display, and store your virtual creations. Use your space to host events, build a business, entertain friends, and have a place to call home. Whatever the motivation, there is a cost to ownership to weigh into your decision. If you decide ownership is not for you or you are hesitant to make that kind of a financial commitment, then Renting may be a good alternative to explore. To enjoy Second Life you DO NOT need land. Only about 15% of the residents actually own land (though another segment rents). You don't have to have land (rent or own) to have fun in Second life.

Converting the Real to Virtual

CHAPTER 18:
LANDING PAD
Finding Your Pasture

Don't Soar Until You Know How to Land

There are many questions that always come up about Owning Land. There's a lot to explain about **Land Management**. In the Information box below we define the various tabs in the Land tool. The more advanced subject of terrain, assigning Prims, group land, private islands, auctions, dividing land parcels and assigning rights is saved for the more established resident and is considered beyond the scope of this book. You have quickly progressed from crawling, to walking, and now to flying...but soaring will have to wait.

INFORMATION: ABOUT LAND

Land Information and Management are handled through the **About Land** tool.

ABOUT LAND: While on the parcel of land. Right-click on the land itself, and select About Land from the pie menu that appears; or left-click World in the menu bar and select **About Land**.

TABS:

GENERAL TAB:
This tab provides basic information about the land including deeds and covenants.

- **Name:** As the land owner you can give the property a name that will display for that parcel. If you choose to register your parcel with the directory listing (for a fee) this name will appear in the **Search** (Ctrl-F) menu under the **Places Tab**.

- **Description:** Additional text to describe your parcel. This description also appears in the directory listing. This field is referenced for the keyword look-up option used in the **Places Tab** of **Search** (Ctrl-F).

- **Owner:** When you purchase the land you are listed here. If you've deeded land to a group, the group name is listed.

INFORMATION: ABOUT LAND (Cont.)

- **Group:** The group that is associated with the land. Click **Set...** button to change the group. Setting land to group, does not deed land to the group. A group setting is used to allow members to build yet restricting others from building.

- **Allow Deed to Group:** Click this and the **Deed...** button to deed the land to the currently selected group.

- **Owner Makes Contribution With Deed:** Check this button to "contribute" your land to the group. Used to take advantage of pooling for a lower tier level (for example, each member contributing their first tier-free 512 sq. meters) and the group also gets a 10% bonus of land to hold under any tier level.

- **Sell For:** Check to set the land for sale at the price you list. It can be sold to a specific person (or anyone if no name is chosen). Check everything twice before you click and close the deal.

- **Sell objects with land:** Option to transfer all of the transferable objects you own at the time the land is purchased. Only objects that display land owners name are included. Click **Show** to see exactly what will be transferred.

- **Claimed:** Date that this parcel was last acquired.

- **Area:** Listing of parcel size in square meters.

- **Traffic:** A tracking of the cumulative time spent by residents on the land in the past day.

- **Buy Land:** Click when you are ready to purchase of the land.

- **Buy for Group:** Click if you are buying the land for a group. The group is listed as the owner of the land. The group has to have the L$ contributions to own land.

- **Buy Pass:** Land is sometimes listed as restricted-access, you can then click this option to buy an access pass. This lets you enter for the amount of time the pass is good for.

- **Release Land:** This option immediately releases you from owner obligation and makes the land public property. It can then be purchased by anyone. Don't release land if you want to keep it or give it to someone else!

INFORMATION: ABOUT LAND (Cont.)

OBJECTS TAB:

Contains information about the objects that are on your land, and on land you own within the region.

- **Simulator Object Usage:** Reflects both the grand sum of Prims on all the plots you own in this region, as well as the total sum allowed on those plots. If you don't own the land, this is the total for that landowner counting all that they own in the region.

- **Objects Parcel Supports:** Shows the number of Prims that can be placed on a single plot of land. If you decide to purchase this land (and add it to what you have in the region) then it is the amount of additional Prim usage you'll gain.

- **Objects on Parcel:** Shows a breakdown (by object owner) of the total number of Prims located on this parcel.

  - **Parcel Owner:** shows the count of Prims the owner placed on the land.

  - **Set to Group:** reflects objects owned by group members that are **Set...** to the associated group.

  - **Owned by Others:** includes objects owned by other people or group members who failed to set the object to the group.

- **Autoreturn:** Objects owned by others (that are not the owner's or associated group members) that are on the parcel after set period of time are returned automatically.

- **Object Owners:** This option displays a list of object owners and you can pick out specific people and return their objects automatically.

OPTIONS TAB:

Setting that determine what can and cannot be done on your land.

- **Create/Edit Objects:** Allows residents to create objects on the land. An owner always has the right to create objects on their land.

- **Safe (no damage)**: This setting makes your land "safe" and no one can "die" here. Usually this is unchecked in areas that allow combat.

INFORMATION: ABOUT LAND (Cont.)

- **Landmark:** Allows residents to create a landmark for future reference.

- **Outside Scripts:** Allows scripts in objects to function when they are on your land. If you uncheck the option it keeps others from doing things like firing weapons.

- **Show in Find Places (L$30/week):** If checked you are charged L$30 a week to be listed in the **Places Search** Window (Ctrl-F). Also select the category you want your land to be listed under (Store, Game, Homestead, etc).

- **Edit Land:** If checked, anyone can terraform the land(change ground and terrain). Keep this unchecked, since as the owner you can always edit your own land.

- **Fly:** Residents can be restricted from flying on your land if you check this option. They can still fly over it but they can't start to fly once they have touched the ground.

- **Outside Scripts:** Allows scripts in objects to function when they are on your land. If you uncheck the option it keeps others from doing things like firing weapons.

- **Snapshot:** This texture picker allows you to choose a picture of your property to display when residents look for you in the Search Directory or Pick your property as a favorite to share in their Profile. Any reference to your land will display this picture.

- **Landing Point:** By selecting a landing point you can control where people will appear when teleporting to your land. Stand where you want the landing point and press **Set** to record it.

INFORMATION: ABOUT LAND (Cont.)

MEDIA TAB:

Controls the sound and video on your land.

- **Restrict spatialized sound to this parcel:** Check this if you don't want sound from outside your parcel to be heard on your parcel. Also, the music and sound from inside your parcel won't spill out.

- **Music URL:** Enter a URL you would like to use to stream music onto your land.

- **Media Texture:** If you use streaming media, this texture will be replaced with the media when the texture is placed on an object. Also enter here any URL you would like to stream media from.

- **Auto Scale Content:** This feature will scale content to better fit into the media texture space. It may slow your media playback and even reduce the quality.

ACCESS TAB:

Allows you to control access to your land.

- **Group:** By checking this then only the members of the group (that you selected in the General Tab) are allowed on the land.

- **Avatars:** When you check this it restricts land access to specific residents that you add to the access list.

- **Sell Passes:** Use when you want people to pay for the right to enter. You can set it for a specified time period.

BAN TAB:

This list of Avatars CANNOT visit your land. They can still fly over the land at a certain height. If people are "Griefing" or abusive you can always *right-click* directly on them, then freeze and eject them.

Everyone is Someone

Owning land allows you to manage and control what happens on that land. You can prevent others from visiting or building there, change the shape of the land, subdivide and sell it, and much more. The **About Land** menu lets you access most of your land's functions, and gives provides you with information about the land you own.

Not everyone is a landowner, a creator, or a techie. Not every Basic Account holder is a griefer or a freeloader. Many people with unverified basic accounts are international residents without access to the credit card or PayPal payment systems offered by Linden Lab. Everyone, though, in Second Life is contributing one way or another. They may be a renter, a consumer, a worker, or simply enjoy the social experience.

So don't feel that you have to own land in Second Life or need to sign up for a premium membership to have a worthwhile experience.

ABOUT LAND TIPS AND HINTS:

- Press P or Ctrl-Alt-Shift-P to see parcel boundary lines. Make sure you know what you're purchasing.

- Take note of the About Land listings for the land's area in square meters.

- Read the **Objects Parcel Supports** Prim amount in About Land under the **Objects** tab. This indicates how many Prims you can place on this land. The **Simulator Object Usage** entry is **NOT** the measure of the Prim allocation since you don't own the land yet and the present owner may own more plots in that sim that is added in.

- When you deed land to a group, you no longer own the land yourself. It is now owned by that group. You receive no money from deeding it. This means the officers of the group can sell, divide, abandon or otherwise change the land and control it.

- Make sure you are happy with the overall shape of the land you want to buy. Some strange shapes are difficult to fit standard builds.

- Be aware of the terrain factor. Most land in Second Life can only be raised 4m above or below its original position, and the previous owner may have raised it already to that limit.

ABOUT LAND TIPS AND HINTS: (Cont.)

- Prims are counted toward your land's Prim count when the center of the object rests in your space

- If the center of the object is on the neighboring land, the tool in the About Land won't recognize the object even though it overhangs onto your land. Therefore you won't be able to use the return tool to remove it.

- If you have an object on your land that belongs to someone else and you are unable to return via the land tools, contact (IM) the owner of the object first and ask to have it removed. Give them some time to respond.

- If the object owner doesn't respond to remove the overhanging object from your land, then ask the owner of the neighboring land to remove the object or one of the group officers if it is group land. You can IM the owner or group members.

- If you have a problem and you have tried everything you can think of to resolve it, then email support@secondlife.com and detail the exact location (region and grid numbers) and clearly describe the problem.

- You can always log in to your Second Life account summary to get information about your tier level and your use fees. Look at your transaction history to see a listing of charges on your account.

- Linden Lab will email you when your monthly tier is being charged against your account.

Consider Thy Neighbor

You are going to have to deal with your neighbors in Second Life whether you like it or not. The only way to get around it would be to buy a private Island that is surrounded by water or void space and live like a hermit. Since Second Life is all about being social, then that defeats the purpose of you being there.

One of the biggest areas of friction is inconsiderate neighbors. When someone pays real money to buy a plot of land, and then the actions of another affects their space, it's natural for them to feel frustrated and compelled to want to do something about it.

Each resident may have their own opinion of what is acceptable and not. But the rule of thumb that is promoted is to do unto others only what you wouldn't mind someone doing to you. So don't invite grief on yourself by being inconsiderate.

EXERCISE 18: BE A GOOD NEIGHBOR

Following are some of the rules of reason we recommend you follow when you are looking to buy (or even rent) land.

- When looking at land, consider your intended purpose for it and how it will fit into the neighborhood.

- If your prospective plot is surrounded by low-build residential housing, then don't put up 50 m pink neon Kitty Kat Club or a shooting gallery with combat zone. If the ownership was reversed, how would you feel?

- Don't erect a 50m wall and block the view of the neighbor behind you on the hill.

- When planting trees, don't place them on the land boundary allowing them to sway into your neighbors house.

- Watch to make sure your light beams and particle streams are not overflowing your property onto the neighbor's space.

- If you are the first to develop a parcel in the area, then those that follow don't have cause to complain.

- Don't open your business directly next door to your major competitor.

- Everyone likes to practice building, but don't let your place look like a sandbox. Finish your builds or take them back into Inventory if you are never going to get around to completing them.

- Be careful of creating lag or lag producing builds. This happens when you use badly written script, unnecessarily large textures on small Prims, or have large parties with tons of bling walking around.

- Watch that your "Camping" isn't becoming an irritant for the region. This is when you pay people to "sit" on your property. It creates for you a high traffic count. However, some regions are restricted to no more than about 40 people in the region at a given time, and if they are all sitting on your property, it closes the region to new people entering. May even make it difficult for people to go home.

- Never build anything that overlaps onto your neighbors land. Try to leave at least a meter or two around the edge of your land.

- Remember Chat (especially shout), music, and media streams will travel across parcel boundaries and affect the quality of your neighbor's space.

- Setting up Ban lines can keep people out of your land to ensure your privacy. However, Ban lines make it difficult often for residents to move around the other properties in the area. Consider a security system instead.

♦ Remember Sky Boxes are not really private (check TOS and CS rules for what you can't do in an M or PG area). You would need a security system of some sort to make it private from camera view.

♦ Never extend any security system control lines over your parcel boundary.

♦ When building sky boxes make sure they are positioned appropriately over only your property. Accidentally crossing over the boundary lines puts added Prim count onto your neighbor.

♦ Don't ban "all Avatars" from your property; it's the equivalent of calling everyone in second life an irritant and a Griefer. It will irritate everyone, even those just flying over.

Remember that retaliation is NEVER the answer. Be creative, often there are solutions you can work with. For example, if the neighbor is an eye sore, put up a phantom wall with your side textured with a beautiful scene.

CHAPTER 19:
ECLECTICALLY SPEAKING
Know it All?

Me, Myself, and I

An alternative (alt) account is a secondary account created by a member. This Avatar has a different name from their primary Avatar. To create an alt account, just sign up through the signup process as you would when creating any other account. You will be asked by Linden Lab if you are setting up an alt account. At least now Linden Lab provides the alts with the option to fast track through Orientation Island, so you don't have to go through the same required exercises each time. There is no direct link between your accounts that is visible to anyone residents. So no one really knows who the alts are. However, disciplinary actions on one account can affect your access to the alt accounts.

Alts are set up for a number of reasons. Sometimes a user wants to be able to move around SL incognito. In other words, if you are publicly active with your Avatar and it can be easily related to you or your work, then you may want a separate Avatar to use for "play" or to make it easier for you to have different creature designs in play.

Alts are also often set up as a Non-Player Character (NPC). This is beyond the scope of this book. It is essentially when an Avatar is set up for the business, to make it easier to keep track of the required accounting.

Whatever the reason, each user is allowed to have five accounts associated with the same credit card and no one needs to know.

Socially Speaking

Socializing takes place in many different settings, ranging from the familiar bars and night clubs, to the slightly more untraditional caves, medieval forests, and gothic castles. The architecture around SL alone can even be more unusual than some of the creatures you run into.

Few regions have building regulations, and residents are able to build whatever their imaginations can garner. Often you will see clashes in architectural styles and themes. This does create some interesting transitions as you fly from one area to the next. As a result some residents have regulated their regions through land covenants and group associations that control the theme in an area in order to effect a more consistent and cooperative flow to regions. Often the desire is that other players will respect their property and their decision.

Really, it's Not Real

Since nothing is really real in SL, unfortunately some people believe then that behavior doesn't matter either. This makes it easy for users to hide behind the anonymity of the Internet. No one expects there is a real dragon behind that creature, or a true fox behind that furry. How about that Warrior who decides to make Second Life a personal combat zone? This causes all sort of emotional feelings to surface on both sides. Then mix it with money, time, and investment, and you end up with some really angry folks.

As a general rule think of every Avatar as having a real person behind it or think of every Avatar as a real person (albeit not their true identity). This helps keep everyone in perspective (at least to some degree). No one, except the dictatorship of Linden Lab can enforce or tell people how to act in Second Life. Having observed the informal rules that seem to work generally in Second Life, we offer up our suggestions on what it takes to successfully cohabitate in this world.

INFORMATION: INFORMAL RULES OF SL

When it comes down to acceptable behavior, everyone usually has their own standard. These suggestions are guidelines to keep SL in perspective, not a comprehensive list, but a good place to start.

MAKE BELIEVE AND ROLE PLAY

- Always remember that not everyone is who they say they are. Men can be women, and women men. Never assume and you won't be upset. Just be cautious if there is an attraction developing.

- Many people are role-playing in Second Life. Some may appear much more obvious than others. If it's not your thing, just ignore them. If it *is* your thing, respect that it may not be someone else's.

- Some people take role playing very seriously and don't appreciate when someone only half-plays. Some communities have key words they use to signal if they are "in role."

- If you are not quite sure what to do in a public situation then sometimes a private side IM to another player can clarify the situation.

- If you are visiting a role-playing or theme region, it's polite to try and do your best to fit in.

- Remember that no one is obligated to play along.

INFORMATION: INFORMAL RULES OF SL (Cont.)

SANDBOXES

- When you build in sandboxes always clean up after yourself.

- Be considerate of others. Don't disturb other residents who are concentrating. Don't crash into people, don't run over things that are not yours, don't create havoc. Don't purposely create lag.

- Don't build or rez objects at the landing point. Teleport in and find another spot.

COMMUNICATIONS

- Don't spam the Chat, residents, or group lists.

- Don't group message when it is more appropriate to talk to people individually (IM).

- Remember not everyone's first language is English so it is best to keep abbreviations and Chat slang at a minimum.

- Don't automatically sweet talk and play up to every good looking Avatar. Remember, the human player may not be the same as the Avatar and may not welcome the advances. Try to get to know Avatars before assuming why they are there.

- Remember if you give out personal information, it is public. If you overhear personal information, you should never pass it along. Each person needs to find their own comfort level in what they are willing to share and with whom.

FRIENDS AND ACQUAINTANCES

- If an Avatar looks like they are staring at you, it may just be they are idle and that's the stance they take. If it bothers you just move away. If the Avatar continues to bother you, teleport away from them.

- Don't jump at making Friends with strangers since they gain the ability to automatically see you online. Give out a calling card instead.

- It's rude to beg for money or items from other players. It's a big NO-NO. Players work for their money, buy it, or receive it through stipends. You need to do the same.

INFORMATION: INFORMAL RULES OF SL (Cont.)

OBJECTS AND ITEMS

- People work hard at developing product so don't expect them to give you a copy free just because you ask nicely. If you do ask and they say NO, don't be surprised.

- Some people do give items away free to help others. These items are usually advertised and marked as such. Some residents give some great builds away, but ask that you respect their wishes to not sell them. Do not abuse the trust that came with the gift.

- Shooting people with weapons is not allowed outside of designated areas. Randomly shooting at people or destroying and disrupting things will earn you an abuse report.

ABUSE

- Report any abuses that you see. Examples include caging people, shooting, pushing, creating lag, blocking entrances, attaching scripts for redirecting payments, stalking, trying to extort money, spamming, using a copybot, leaving objects that attack, or doing anything that can create problems with the grid.

Linden Dollars

Second Life residents use a currency called the Linden Dollars (L$). The official exchange is called the LindeX, however there are outside exchanges that are also brokering these dollars for US$ or other currency. These exchanges have been precipitated by the restrictions imposed by Linden Lab on volume trades and waiting periods. Also, there is money to be made on these transactions so it makes sense that third party exchanges have grown.

Check your account on the Second Life website under the heading **Billing and Trading Limits** to see what your maximum buy and sell orders are set at. A new account (basic or premium) is limited in the first 30 days. Typically in the first week you can only buy up to a maximum of US$50 in Lindens and can't sell any back. Then in the first 30 days it is raised to a US$150 with US$300 equivalent to sell back.

Another 30 day restriction imposed on Newbies is how much that can actually be purchased from Linden Lab when you add up membership, lindens, tier fees, and anything else for dollars. So pay attention if you have some aggressive plans in your first 30 days.

A large portion of the residents have no way to earn money other than buying it with money from outside, and those who earn large amounts of money often only do so in order to sell it for money from outside. So you will hear complaints from consumers that a rising L$ gives them bad value for their US$, and sellers will complain that a falling L$ gives them bad return on their work.

Internationally Speaking

At the last reporting from Linden Lab: 99% of the Active residents represented 100 different countries. "Active" meaning they logged in for an hour or more in the month being counted. The top 10 included the United States (31%), France (13%), Germany (10.5%), United Kingdom (8%), Netherlands (7%), Spain (4%), Brazil (4%), Canada (3%), Belgium (3%), and Italy (2%).

As with real world users, bi-lingual Second Life has been exploding. Now Linden Lab is adding more language options to Second Life, which could further expand it's market exponentially. Anyone with a computer, the SL tools, and the desire, could become an entrepreneur.

Linden Lab has already converted their website to German, Korean, and Japanese language options. It's also rumored that Chinese will soon follow.

MONEY TIPS AND HINTS:

♦ Exchange Rates will fluctuate so sometimes its worth it to shop around. Often the outside rates for buying Linden Dollars are more attractive than the Official Linden Exchange rate.

♦ LindeX charges a fixed fee of $0.30 per transaction regardless of the amount of L$ you purchase.

♦ Sellers on LindeX are presently charged 3.5% per transaction. The net dollars then are credited to your US$ account balance.

♦ There are other fees associated with transferring money by check processing or PayPal. Check the Second Life web site for details. The same for any other exchanges. Check their fee schedules.

MONEY TIPS AND HINTS: (Cont.)

- Linden Lab will accept credit cards, PayPal, domestic and international checks. The fees and waiting period will vary.

- There are higher maximums on the L$ that can be bought and sold once Linden Lab classifies your account as a Business, Enterprise, or Currency Trader.

- We have seen the Premium Membership stipend fall (L$500 to L$300); although, so far, each account is still receiving the stipend they had in effect at their sign-up. It's just lower for the newer accounts.

Reach Out and Touch Someone

It's not uncommon to meet individuals, groups, or communities that speak different languages. As a result, residents are attempting to bridge communication hurdles in a number of creative ways. For example, translation HUDs have been developed and are being sold in-world. Now an Avatar can wear one on their screen to communicate in nearly any language.

All you have to do is type in one language and select the language you want it translated into on your screen. Simply don the device, set the language you'll be typing in, and the different one that you want will appear on screen. Language classes and translation services are readily offered as well. Then, of course, the language of Building is universal. Second Life is definitively positioned to transcend the real world geographic boundaries.

Earn a Living or Two

Second life offers opportunities. Everywhere you look. Whether it is working for someone or becoming self-employed, a good part of "life" in-world is contributing to it. Most residents have not given up their real life day job. However, more and more residents are finding ways of blending the two. Whether you choose to work two jobs, integrate a real life job into an SL one, or make a second life business career jump, there seems to always be opportunity to serve this robust economy and exponential growing market.

EXERCISE 19: MAKE SOME MONEY

Second Life presents you with an endless variety of ways to spend your Linden Dollars, but supporting your lavish lifestyle will eventually mean deciding on a way to earn some as well.

How much you need to make in Second Life will depend upon whether you are trying to make a Second Life level of earnings or a Real World earnings.

FREE MONEY

As a Newbie, you may need some pocket change. The best way to make money some quick money is to search the classifieds for **Free Money** and look for the following keywords:

♦ **MoneyTree:** These are trees that grow L$ but are only available to new Avatars (for example, less than 30 days old)

♦ **Camping Chairs:** They are available to anyone. Their purpose is to pay you to sit in the chair for as long as possible so that the land traffic goes up.

♦ **Surveys:** Some firms are legitimate business concerns and truly want an opinion, others are solely collecting your name and email address for spamming. Pick carefully.

Opinions are Important
(Courtesy of SurveysXpress)

EVENTS AND CONTESTS

Sometimes the Lindens and others will run events that provide new residents (and others) opportunities to win money. Common are Theme Building Competitions, Dance Contests, Best Dressed Contests, Show and Tell, and Races.

SECOND LIFE PAY

A Second Life earning may or may not make you enough money to pay for your membership, buy land, or pay tiers. It can make you enough to enjoy the game with a Basic Membership. It just depends on how much effort you want to put into this livelihood.

UNSKILLED LABOR JOBS

These are found in the classifieds. Typically requires a little training but virtually no skill. These added funds can help keep you in clothes or pay your rent.

- ◆ **Greeters, Hosts, and Attendants:** Paid to be sociable, friendly, add traffic, and watch property for the casino, owner, or event. These jobs provide customer service and watch for abuse.

- ◆ **Adult Entertainment Hosts, Dancers, Strippers, and Floor Managers.** This is a Mature category that supports the Adult Entertainment Business of dancing, performing, and anything goes for money.

- ◆ **Receptionists, Security, Sales Associates:** For a variety of businesses.

SKILLED JOBS

To start making money that's closer to real life pay (albeit minimum wage) requires a lot more time, commitment, ingenuity, and skill. It also means building relationships with the people you meet in-world. Below are some of the categories of "jobs" that can be found.

- • **Receptionists, Sales Associates, and Event Planners**

- • **DJs, Musicians, and Performers**

- • **Reseller, Product Distributor, or Network Promoter**

- • **Instructors, News Reporters, and Writers**

- • **Building, Landscaping and Interiors**

- • **Scripting and Software Support**

Make Something of Yourself

You'll also find that Second Life offers a lot of opportunity for the entrepreneur. Second Life has a healthy economy where residents trade both goods and services. Combining ingenuity and skill, you can be Second Life's next big real estate developer, top fashion designer, weapons manufacturer, advertising agency, distributor, or musician. Other ideas that have been developed include:

Make Something to Sell

In Second Life the opportunity for a bigger and better mousetrap always will exist. Look for ideas, improve on the ones out there, Create and build things like jewelry, vehicles, skyscrapers, prefab houses, furniture, casino games, flexi-hair, shoes, plants, weapons, watches, signs, boats, and even new bodies.

To sell an item, just select it, choose edit, and check off the "for sale" box and name your price. If you own land, you can place your creations there to display, or you can make a deal with another resident to help you sell your item in their store.

Make Something of Someone Else

Real life, multi-national type, companies have started invading Second Life. They are just starting to figure out how to tap into the market potential it has to offer.

Companies like Toyota, General Motors, Dell, Cisco, Sun Microsystems, IBM, Adidas, and AOL are embracing the online world to advertise, test products and market ideas. Second Life offers an inexpensive marketing avenue with the potential of astronomical reach.

Some companies are linking Second Life visitors to their real-world e-commerce Web sites. Others like Wal-Mart, Intel, and American Express are investigating avenues of integrating their real businesses with virtual worlds. All are recognizing that these virtual worlds are a wave worth riding.

Let's not forget that SL is making inroads in every imaginable direction. Increasingly we are seeing universities, educational institutions, non-profit organizations, charities, and government agencies joining the ranks. Every time you look around, or read the press, familiar products, people, and organizations have adopted a Second Life. (See Appendix for a sample list in the Explore SL Recommendations).

As you develop your skill and knowledge of Second Life, you are in a position to open the door for helping others step into the world either through a business interest, educational endeavor, a personal friendship, or simply game-playing fun. Don't underestimate what you can do since you have now crossed over from being a Newbie to an experienced player.

CHAPTER 20:
TAG YOU'RE "IT"
No Longer a Newbie Now

Leader of the Pack

Even though everyone says relax and have fun with Second Life, it can be an unnerving experience to be in unfamiliar surroundings. It's easy to get embarrassed when you fall on your face in landing or when you accidentally wear a box, or have trouble unpacking items. It's natural not to want to make a mistake or look like a fool, even though no one really knows who you are. You don't really know what to expect when you step out of the protective Orientation environment. Exactly what are you truly in for? And for some of us, that first experience may not have been so friendly with rude people sometimes lurking around.

It's very easy to forget that there are actual people behind the assortment of Avatars you'll encounter in your quest, but it's true. Most people you will encounter sincerely want to be friendly and helpful, if for no other reason than to help others because they appreciated it when they were new.

Remember you never know who you will meet and where connections and friendships may lead, not to mention the good karma gained from helping others. That poor Newbie with the box on his head, the white underwear outfit, and the nerdy glasses may end up being someone prominent in SL in the future, and you know them. In fact, you may end up dating them, working for them, or even building an empire with them. At the very least, if you meet a Newbie, help them to transcend that cavernous first step into Second Life.

Extend Yourself

To become skilled in Second Life means you have to extend yourself beyond your comfort zone. What that means is that you have to put out a little effort. Use the list below to pick out one new thing you will do each session to stretch your horizon and skill.

Here is our suggestion list. Choose a different thing to try each time. Stick with it, at least attempt to get through one of the suggestions in each category. You don't have to become accomplished at it, just try it out.

TRY SOMETHING NEW... EVERYDAY!

EXPERIMENT

This means you are going to pick a tool that you haven't used and try it out. Even a tool we haven't really discussed. You have a lot to choose from. You can select something randomly from the Menu Bar at the top of your screen, or you can choose an option in one of the Buttons on the bottom of your screen. Here are some ideas in case you can't think of anything:

Try Planting Some Trees. Using the Library folder in Inventory, bring out some trees (1 Prim each). See what trees you can plant on your land or the Sandbox by also using the Create (Ctrl-4) shapes. There is grass and trees there for planting as well. Try them out. Notice the Prim count.

Play with Gestures. Find the gestures in the Library, in your freebie stuff, and on the bottom of your screen. Experiment with using them.

Try Making a Movie. Experiment with the movie to disc (Ctrl-Shift-A) feature. When you are finished see if you can get it to play back (it will depend on what software you have on your computer for this function).

Open the Statistics Bar (Ctrl-Shift-1). See if you can make sense of it. The command keys will toggle it on and off.

Explore Preferences. *Left-click* **Edit** in the Menu Bar to find it. Familiarize yourself with what's there. You actually may want to change some of those settings.

EXPLORE A NEW PLACE

If you haven't used the recommended Keyword searches that we gave you in some of the previous chapters, then go back and do that. You can also look in the Appendix for even more locations to explore. Pick out some you haven't visited yet. Another place to go is the Search tool (Ctrl-F) and using the **Places Tab**, randomly put in keywords related to your interests and see what you come up with; or look at the **Popular Place** list and find something of interest.

TRY SOMETHING NEW... EVERYDAY! (Cont.)

TAKE A CLASS

There are a bunch of classes you can find around Second Life that are free. Look at the Events listing in the Search tool (Ctrl-F). Also when in-world use the Help (F1) key and you can find a list of Upcoming Classes. Try the search directly with your browser by going to www.eventful.com. Instead of filling in your City, type in "Second Life." Besides the popular Build classes, there are classes on everything from Spanish to Machinima to Feung Shui. It doesn't have to be a Second Life skill, just seeing how things are done is a class in itself.

ASK QUESTIONS

Don't be afraid to ask questions. People love to share their knowledge, and the SL residents are no different. Just ASK. It doesn't have to be anywhere in particular. If you are in a casino, ask how to play the games. In a class, speak up (or stay after). IM people from the groups you joined (use group talk here sparingly, IM them individually). When you're shopping, ask questions of the store keepers or even other shoppers. Ask, ask, ask. You will be amazed at how much you will learn this way.

READ SOMETHING...ANYTHING

Tons of stuff is available on the web. There are Blogs, there are Newsletters, Forums, Fansites, etc. Read and familiarize yourself with the Second Life website. Look at our **Website Resources List** in the Appendix. Visit Linden Village, New Citizens Plaza, and the Tower of Prims and you will find things to read on about everything in Second Life. Just search the web and pages of sources will appear.

JOIN OR PARTICIPATE IN SOMETHING

You probably have an interest, hobby, or profession in real life. Search for Second Life Groups that share the same interest. This is easy to do by using the Search tool for **Groups**. Also, don't overlook the **Places** and **Events** tabs as other great sources to hook into things to join or participate in. There is always something going on in SL. Even LL has in-world events that they sponsor in SL. Look and you shall find.

No Longer a Newbie Now

So you made it. You've covered a lot of territory in a short period of time, and surprisingly if you lasted this long, you probably have a thirst for more. So now what? Since the world (SL that is) keeps evolving, you've got the challenge of keeping up. Practice a little more; pursue some of your passions; continue to meet people; set aside time to explore; plus watch, and learn.

That's your new challenge as you carve out and form your piece of Second Life to be whatever you want it to be. Want to find out more? Spend a few minutes trying to learn something new at each in-world session. You can explore and try out some of the menu options you haven't used yet, or take a class exploring new tools that you've never used before in-world. Ask questions of fellow residents to understand what they mean, or search the Knowledge Base or Official Blogs to see what other features LL has to offer. It's worth overcoming any fears and doubts you might have and ask questions, make suggestions, and have your voice heard. You'll be glad you did.

If you don't consider yourself adventurous or a pioneer, let us let you in on a secret. We were all new at one time. We didn't give in, but instead forged (or should I say trudged) ahead. Looking back at the experience I've got to admit it was worth it and the satisfaction in the accomplishments made felt tremendously great.

Yep, you are a pioneer. You're riding a wave of change. Can't you feel it? In addition to the educational impact being created by Second Life, there are a rapidly growing number of universities, businesses, news agencies, non-profit organizations, technology and healthcare entities, and a number of widely-diverse interest groups active with Second Life. Virtual campuses are merging the tools of technology with the tools of education to prepare for meeting the world's future needs and expectations.

The world of tomorrow has arrived and it is virtually here today.

—Tara Anna

APPENDIX

TAKE THE QUICK FLIGHT ACTIVITY CHALLENGE

SECOND LIFE TRIVIA AND FACTS

EASY COMMAND GUIDE

SL INFORMATION VENUES

WEBSITE RESOURCES

SL EXPLORE RECOMMENDATIONS

QUICK REFERENCE TERMS

DEFINITION OF COMMON TERMS

SCREEN COMMANDS

TAKE THE QUICK FLIGHT ACTIVITY CHALLENGE

Here is a list of 13 activities you can do at the ArcheBooks Bookstore Property; Taesot (169, 47, 117). Let's see how much you've learned.

Can you complete the List?

1. Join the "**Quick Flight Book Group**" and we will send you Holiday Greeting Cards throughout the year. These cards are Copy/Transfer for your own use and distribution. We will also provide you with update notifications.

2. Play the Piano in **The Ricardo Group Office Complex** Lobby.

3. Visit **v3image** Office on the 2nd floor of the Office Building for a copy of our latest Gift Box of Freebies.

4. Browse the **Archebooks Bookstore** for Original Works of Fiction. Pick up a sample book from one of the authors.

5. Visit Dagmar in the backyard behind **Archebooks Bookstore**. Find him near his doghouse.

6. Post your favorite SL Tour Itinerary to share (Chapter 16). Add it to the **Tour Board** at the **SL World Tours** Office. Browse the board if you are looking for more locations to explore.

7. Take the SurveyXpress **Book Review Survey** in the Central Square and receive Linden Dollars (L$).

8. Enter the **v3image Photo Journey Contest**. Deposit your boxed photos into the Contest Box located inside the **Photo-Art Gallery**. (Rules and Photo requirements in Chapter 13).

9. Watch for the **Photo-Art Gallery** display of the **Photo Journey Contest Winners** Published Works.

10. Pose in the **Photo Studio** and take your own Portrait.

11. Post an Idea for Book 2 on the *PostNet* IDEA BOARD.

12. Stroll through the **Art Gallery** featuring an Original Artist and pick up a brochure. If you are an Artist, drop off a box of your art work with a brochure (provide full permissions) for the rotated display.

13. **Instant Message (IM) Reada Dailey** and send her your self-portrait (full permissions please) when you've completed this Entire Activity Challenge. Your picture will be added to the **Challenge Board** display located on property.

*****Quick Flight** refers to your rapid advancement from Newbie to seasoned resident.

SECOND LIFE TRIVIA AND FACTS

• On U.S. Holidays look to the sun and moon. They are often overlaid with custom textures for the holidays. Past sightings include Easter eggs, Valentine Heart; Halloween Man in the Moon Face, Three Leaf Clover.

• On October 18, 2006 the sun and moon texture reflected the 1 million resident population milestone that was reached.

• April 1st (April Fool's Day) is always a day to look for strange things happening in Second Life. Odd things are guaranteed to occur. Sometimes humorous and other times just strange. Keep your eyes open because it is hard to say what to expect.

• A Second Life day is 4 hours long, with 3 hours of daytime and 1 hour of night. What that means, we really don't know except that it is the pattern of the odd daylight and nighttime occurrences.

• The sun orbits the SL world and travels faster during the night. Obviously since night is only an hour. Notice that the moon is always full.

• Linden Lab has moved office locations 3 times. The first location was 333 Linden Street, the second was on Second Street, and the third and current location is 1100 Sansome Street, San Francisco, CA.

• The Hippo is called the unofficial but official mascot of Second Life. SL National Hippo Day is celebrated on Febuary 15th!

• Linden is also the name of a tree. In Britain it is called a "lime" tree and is sometimes also called a "basswood".

• Steller Sunshine was the first SL resident ever (Born: 3/13/2002) when SL was still in alpha. She was an early builder. She is known for building the Governor's Mansion, a tree house and a large beanstalk as early builds in SL.

• The first Beta Regions to come online (November 2002) were named after alleys near the Linden Lab office in San Francisco.

• Several real government communities have been formed, like the Democratic Republic of Neualtenburg.

• Government as we know it is basically nonexistent in SL other than what is referred to as the "dictatorship" of the creator Linden Lab.

• Second Life Time (SLT) was always listed on the SL screen but was the same as Pacific Standard Time (PST). Since it was confusing, Linden Lab decided to call it what it is, "Pacific Standard Time".

• Did you know that the word "Avatar" is a Sanskrit term meaning descent of a deity from heaven?

- The Governor Linden Avatar is actually different Linden Lab employees. It is considered a Non-player character (NPC). You will notice that Governor Linden holds the Linden-protected land and owns a number of builds around SL. Governor Linden is hardly ever seen, but has been represented as a female with purple hair.

- Linden bears are creations of the Linden Staff and some noted residents too. They are collectibles that come in different sizes, shapes, colors, and sometimes reflect special occasions and events. You can find these bears at some of the Linden stations and events. You can also just directly ask the creators (Lindens) for them.

- Since Second Life is considered a World onto itself, LL has encouraged the creation of SL-specific holidays. Presently we've noted SL Holidays include <u>Talk Like A Pirate Day</u>, <u>Hippo Day</u>, <u>Burning Life</u>, and <u>Winter Celebration</u>.

EASY COMMAND GUIDE

WORLD
World Map*   Ctrl-M
Mini Map*   Ctrl-Shift-M
Noon   Ctrl-Shift-Y
Sunset   Ctrl-Shift-N

INFORMATION
on Avatars   *Right-click:* **Profile**
on Objects   *Right-click:* **Edit**
on Land   *Right-click:* **About Land**
on File Item   *Right-click:* **Properties**

COMMUNICATIONS
Chat History*   Ctrl-H
Instant Message*   Ctrl-T
Say *(20 m)*   Enter
Shout *(100 m)*   Ctrl-Enter
No Hands   "/" *(then message)*

VIEW
Search*   Ctrl-F
Mouselook*   M
Reset View   esc *(for mouselook)*

View Around   Alt-*move* cursor
Pan Around   Ctrl-Alt *move* cursor
Reset View   *press* arrow key

Friends List*   Ctrl-Shift-F

FILE
Open Inventory*   Ctrl-I
Select   Ctrl-A
Deselect   Ctrl-D
Copy   Ctrl-C
Paste   Ctrl-V

PICTURES
Upload Image   Ctrl-U
Take Snapshot   Ctrl-Shift-S
Snapshot to disc   Ctrl-'
(Save frame directly to your computer)

Movie to disc*   Ctrl-Shift-A
(Start filming to your computer)

MOVEMENT
Fly*   Shift-F
Gestures*   Ctrl-G
Teleport Home   Ctrl-Shift-H

BUILD
Build*   B
Focus   Ctrl-1
Move   Ctrl-2
Edit   Ctrl-3
Create   Ctrl-4
Land   Ctrl-5

EDIT FUNCTIONS
Link   Ctrl-L
Unlink   Ctrl-Shift-L
Drag Select   *Left-drag*
Group Select   **Shift,** *Left-click*
Move Object   *Left-drag* arrow
Copy Object   Ctrl-D
    Shift-*drag* arrow
Rotate Object   Ctrl-*drag* curve
Stretch Object   Ctrl-Shift *drag* a box
Undo   Ctrl-Z
(Only once while in Edit & Chat window off)

TAB CONTROLS
Next Tab   Ctrl-]
Previous Tab   Ctrl-[

Close Window   Ctrl-W
(works for IM, Friends, Landmarks, Notes)

SL Help   F1
Quit (Exit SL)   Ctrl-Q

PC USERS	MAC USERS
Ctrl	Cmd
Alt	Opt
Shift (same)	Shift (same)
Right-click	*Right-click*
	(Cmd-*click* for a single button mouse)

MAC: A multi-button mouse with a scroll is highly recommended for Second Life.

Note that an upper case letter is actually the lower case key on your keyboard.
**Commands turn the function on and off*

SL INFORMATION VENUES

Linden Lab lists the following resources for further communication with your fellow residents both in SL-World and in the Real World. This list is dynamic, so expect with time that additional resources will probably replace some of those already listed here.

SECOND LIFE RESOURCES

Billboards

Informational postings about events. **Located at various Linden Locations.**

Help (F1)

Quick access to basic information. **Use the F1 Key while in SL.**

Information Kiosks

Network system providing Info on topics. **Look for blue i's on the SL World Map.**

In-world Announcements

Infrequently occur but used to inform of grid troubles and other timely notices. Often offers a Blog link when it appears. **Blue Pop-ups in right corner of your screen.**

Linden Village

SL Official Office where you can find employees to speak to and share some of your ideas. **Search: Linden Village.**

Message of the Day

Provides Hints, Ideas, and late breaking news. **Appears at log-in and found on the SL website.**

Town Halls

Meetings open to the general public. Transcript of meetings are posted on the SL Blog. **Watch for the Announcements.**

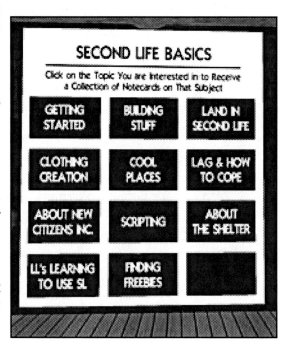

Volunteer Programs, Meetings, and Portal

LL has a volunteer support force for gathering, haring and disseminating information. **http://wiki.secondlife.com/wiki/Volunteer_Portal**

REAL LIFE RESOURCES

Feature Voting Tool
Propose things for SL and it's posted for LL comments and vote.
http://secondlife.com/vote/

Forums
Forums are sorted into categories and used primarily for Resident-to-Resident help.
Linden Forums: Official Information
Classified Forums: Sell, Rent, Need Help
Discussion Forums: Ideas, Questions, Debate
Group Forums: For Groups only discussions
http://forums.secondlife.com/

Knowledge Base
Search data base for information about how to do things in Second Life.
http://secondlife.com/knowledgebase/

Official Linden Blog
Official announcements and resident comments.
http://blog.secondlife.com

Known Issues
List of the latest bugs discovered.
http://secondlife.com/support/known-issues.php

Mailing Lists
eMail networks by Interest type. Sign up and get involved communicating with like minds.
http://secondlife.com/community/mailinglists.php

Public Bug Tracker
Open report and comments on bugs, pooling of knowledge to resolve issues.
https://jira.secondlife.com/

Second Life Wiki
Interactive resident driven data base. Allows you to edit and contribute. Search for information on SL. **http://wiki.secondlife.com/wiki/Main_Page**

The Second Opinion
Official Community Newsletter
http://forums.secondlife.com/

WEBSITE RESOURCES

In addition to Linden Lab and Second Life sponsored resources, there are a number of other venues available to support you in living Second Life. Again, this is not a comprehensive list, but is provided to help you source additional information and pursue further exploration.

CORE WEB SITES

Linden Lab
Creators of Second Life
www.LindenLab.com

Second Life
Membership Site for the Main Grid
www.SecondLife.com

ArcheBooks Publishing, Inc.
Publisher of this book
www.ArcheBooks.com

v3image
Authors of this book and RL/SL Developers
www.v3image.com

LINDEN $ EXCHANGE

Lindex Exchange
Official Linden Dollar Exchange
(located within the Second Life website)
www.secondlife.com

PRODUCT EXCHANGES

SL Exchange
Buy and Sell in SL
www.slexchange.com

SL Boutique
Products to Buy (and Sell)
www.slboutique.com

PHOTO AND VIDEO POSTING

Photo Bucket
Free posting of photos available
www.photobucket.com

Snapzilla
Offers sending a postcard as a posting option.
www.slpics.com

SL Buzz
Postcard posting option and more
www.SLBuzz.com

WEBSITE RESOURCES (Cont.)

MISCELLANEOUS
SL Events Listing
Use to Search Events in SL
www.eventful.com

SL History Wiki
All sorts of good historical info on SL
http://slhistory.org/index.php/Main Page

SL Universe
Third Party Community Site
Forums, Knowledge Base, etc.
www.sluniverse.com

NEWSLETTERS/NEWS SOURCES
Second Opinion
Official news source of SL
www.secondopinion.com

Second Life Insider
www.secondlifeinsider.com

Second Life Herald
www.secondlifeherald.com

SLURL SUPPORT
SLURL
Make SLurls
www.SLurl.com

Tiny URLs
Make lengthy SLURLS short
www.tinyurl.com

TEXTURE SOURCES
Texturama
(Commercial and Free)
Tileable and Quality Textures
www.Texturama.com

Absolute Background Textures
Collection of Free textures
http://www.grsites.com/textures/

Mayangs Free Textures
High Resolution Free Textures
http://www.mayang.com/textures/

SL EXPLORE RECOMMENDATIONS

(Use the **Map** Button (Ctrl-M) and fill in the SL address noted below)

If Coordinates are not listed, then type in only the Region. Note that the names, locations, and owners of these builds do change. This is not a comprehensive listing, nor may it be the best representation of its category. This information is provided solely to guide the reader into categories and areas for exploration. The recommendations are not listed in any particular order.

INFORMATION AND NEWBIE FRIENDLY LOCATIONS

New Citizens Plaza	Kuula (54, 175, 29)
Tower of Prim	Natoma (210, 164, 27)
The Shelter	Swinside (220, 104, 41)
Linden Village	Kirkby (177, 209, 45)
Help Island - Public	Help Island Public (125, 124, 27)
Caledon Tourism & Hospitality Ctr	Caledon II (63, 185, 23)
HealthInfo Island	Healthinfo Island (129, 139, 23)
ICT Library	Info Island (52, 202, 34)

SANDBOX AND PUBLIC SPACES

Combat Sandbox-Linden Lab	Rausch
Six Vehicle Sims-Lnden Lab	Balance, Bethel, Briliant, Fame, Fortuna, and Georgean.
Public Sandbox	Mauve (116, 95, 35)
Azure Islands Aquatic Sandbox!	Aquatic Sandbox (82, 82, 28)
Public Sandbox	Sandbox Island Extension (128, 128)

THEME BUILDS

Castle Blackmoor	Stillman (30, 170)
Luskwood	Lusk (193, 101, 52)
Tehama Piazza Park	Tehama (122, 119, 23)
Galapagos National Park & Wildlife Refuge	Haenim (77, 198, 64)
Caledon Academy of Virtual Wizardry	Caledon Highlands (150, 210, 39)
Tol Eressea	Tol Eressea (2, 2, 0)

SL EXPLORE RECOMMENDATIONS (Cont.)

MUSEUMS AND LANDMARKS

Beta Contributor Wall	Plum (128, 53)
Governor's Mansion	Clementina (176, 118)
Star Trek Museum of Science	Ocean Pines (32, 232, 25)
The Great Wall of SL	Athetis
Eric Linden Bridge	Kissling (159, 199, 69)
Lisbon Opera House	Lanercost
International Spaceflight Museum	Spaceport Alpha (47, 77, 24)
Revelations Tarot Card Museum	Hantu (212, 99, 30)
SL Computer History Museum	Info Island II (241, 54, 23)
The Second Life Planetarium	Spaceport Alpha (24, 53, 23)
Pomponio volcano	Pomponio (97, 221, 96)
The Second Louvre Museum	Tompson (153, 97, 100)

SHOPPING, PRODUCTS, AND MALLS

Freebie Warehouse	Burns (95, 148, 79)
Depoz West	Depoz W (253, 92, 26)
Lego Land Kids Mall	Mullett (207, 134, 146)
Carducci	Coburg (50, 250, 150)
Abranimations	Isere (52, 151, 135)
Black Market/Public Graffiti Project	Sistiana (8, 16 ,0)
Ricx's Fine Jewelry	Nepessing (59,98,125)
Home Sweet Homes	Home Sweet Homes (129,128, 23)
Free Dove	Gallii (113, 53, 33)
DarkDharma Avatar Isle	Dacia (230, 29)
Prefab Alley	Alira (128, 128, 0)
BHE ~ Welcome Center	King of Hearts (128, 100, 28)
Millions' Marble Mall	Westport (231, 105, 62)
Midnight City	Midnight City (114, 141, 28)
B-Dazzled Designs	B Dazzled Island (35, 141, 41)
Perfect Prefabs	Perfect Prefabs Cyan (127, 128, 26)

SL EXPLORE RECOMMENDATIONS (Cont.)

VEHICLES AND TRANSPORTATION

Busy Ben's	Oak Grove
Phase 5 HQ - Airfield	Caldbeck (190, 153, 40)
G-AXIS	Igbo (79, 234, 351)
Virgin Isle Marina	Virgin Isle Marina (53, 52, 24)
Abbotts Aerodrome	Abbotts (160, 152, 71)
Periwinkle Railway Station	Periwinkle (58, 92, 27)
Fierrens Yachts Marina.	Yora (186, 131, 24)
Olive - Great Second Life Rail Way	Olive (246, 186, 41)

UNIVERSITIES, EDUCATION, AND TRAINING

Academy of Second Learning (ASL)	Eson (32, 162, 351)
Glidden Campus	Glidden (153, 163, 27)
Brainiac HQ	Afton (48, 95, 117)
Cisco Campus	Cisco Systems (132, 132, 34)
Ohio University	Ohio University (20, 36, 24)
Talis Cybrary City	Cybrary City (126, 171, 25)
USC Annenberg Island	Annenberg Island (187, 67, 40)
Democracy Island	Democracy Island (156, 174, 27)
Kent State University Salem	Provincetown (226, 157, 31)
RMIT - Ormond Island	RMIT (192, 64, 39)
SDSU Second Life Pioneers	Meadowbrook (220, 83, 23)
Syddansk Universitet	Sabra (9, 180, 94)
UTD ATEC Island	UTD ArtTech Island (137, 51, 37)
Woodbury University Campus	Campus North (136, 9, 24)

GOVERNMENT AND AGENCIES

Neualtenburg Projekt	Neualtenburg (67, 98, 27)
Capitol Hill North	Capitol Hill 1 (102, 4, 30)
Centers for Disease Control (CDC)	Juwangsan (217, 220, 61)
National Oceanic & Atmospheric Administration	Meteroa (246, 244, 309)

SL EXPLORE RECOMMENDATIONS (Cont.)

INTERNATIONAL AND VIRTUAL LOCATIONS

!ILHA BRASIL SAO PAULO JARDINS	Brasil Sp Jardins (64, 125, 26)
Gaia, Accueil francophone	Gaia (226, 62, 34)
Parioli Rome Italy	Parioli (99, 137, 40)
French Sim	Gaia (226, 62, 34)
Rue d'Alliez	Rue d'Alliez (9, 75, 22)
San Francisco (M)	Anarchia (181, 123, 17)
The MonteCarlo Hotel & Casino (M)	Goddess of Love4 (118, 10, 22)
Venice Beach	Venice Beach (70, 116, 25)

RELIGION AND SPIRITUAL LOCATIONS

Church of Second Life (Christian)	Zerelia (38, 250, 97)
St. Nicholas Avatarian Orthodox Church	Mieum (177, 169, 85)
The Jewish Historical Museum and Synagogue	Cuscus (46, 122, 89)
Second Life Catholic Church Information	Huin (138, 181, 125)
A Latter-day Peace Garden	Otaki Gorge (42, 172, 73)

NON-PROFIT LOCATIONS

Techsoup.org	Info Island (66, 184, 33)
Global Kids On The Main Grid	Cincta (80, 105, 32)
EdTech Island	EdTech (100, 133, 25)
World Vision	Kiwa Northwest (53, 169, 24)
The Big Easy - New Orleans recreated for Charity	Big Easy (165, 217, 26)
Creative Commons	Kula (4 39, 35, 21)
Cystic Fibrosis Education	Boomer Island (80, 66, 30)
Genocide Intervention Network, Camp Darfur	Better World (176, 245, 21)
Premiere Urgence, International Humanitarian Aid	Porcupine (131, 150, 117)
Save the Children	Midnight City (34, 220, 26)

SL EXPLORE RECOMMENDATIONS (Cont.)

ENTERTAINMENT AND ACTIVITIES

Ocean Casino & Mall	Plush Epsilon (129,166, 23)
Blackcat Amusement Park	Tajmahal (47, 98, 22)
Koreshan Pointe	Koreshan (242, 79, 24)
Laka Lounge & Resort	Laka
Saphira	Saphira (128,128, 0)
SKY CLUB	Chapala (196, 186, 248)
Ethereal Teal	Teal (128, 128, 30)

REAL LIFE MEDIA COMPANIES

BBC Radio	BBC Radio 1 (128, 127, 32)
CNET	Millions of Us (226, 30, 38)
MTV Laguna Beach	Laguna Beach (63, 218, 25)
NBC Universal Headquarters	NBC 2 (131, 123, 43)
Northsound Radio Scotland	Fusion Unity (204, 131, 22)
Popular Science	Millions of Us (193, 133, 24)
Reuters	Reuters (127, 99, 25)
Sundance Channel	Sundance Channel (55, 173, 38)
The Infinite Mind	Infinite Mind (209, 76, 46)
Wired	Millions of Us (203, 228, 23)

SL EXPLORE RECOMMENDATIONS (Cont.)

REAL LIFE CORPORATIONS AND BRAND NAMES

Adidas	Adidas (104, 183, 55)
American Apparel	Lerappa (138, 92, 24)
AOL Pointe	AOL Pointe (128, 128, 0)
Bantam Dell Publishing	Sheep Island (123, 28, 25)
BMW	BMW New World (195, 66, 23)
Circuit City	IBM 10 (136, 38, 22)
Cisco Systems	Cisco Systems (128, 127, 30)
Dell Computer	Dell Island (43, 162, 24)
H&R Block	HR Block (113, 48, 37)
IBM Sandbox	IBM (121, 154, 33)
Leo Burnett	Millions of Us (193, 80, 23)
Major League Baseball	Baseball (214, 129, 27)
Mercedes-Benz	Mercedes Island(128, 128,0)
Nissan	Nissan (19, 129, 26)
Pontiac Main Island	Pontiac (179, 96, 24)
Reebok	Reebok (111, 100, 97)
Reuters	Reuters (127, 98, 25)
Sears	IBM 10 (95, 32, 23)
Sony/BMG	Media Island (108, 111, 21)
Starwood Hotels	Aloft Island (68, 69, 27)
Sun Microsystems	Sun Pavilion (182, 144,55)
Thompson NetG	Thompson (182, 123, 35)
Toyota	Scion City (44, 40, 23)
Vodafone	Vodafone Island (128, 128,0)
Toyota	Scion City (44, 40, 23)
Vodafone	Vodafone Island (128, 128,0)

QUICK REFERENCE TERMS

CHAT LANGUAGE
(Shortcuts used in Chat)

afk: away from keyboard
alt: alter ego (2nd Avatar account)
asap: As soon as possible
av: Avatar
brb: be right back
btw: By the way
cya: See ya
dba: Doing business as
fyi: For your information
home: base location
k: Okay
kiss: Keep it simple stupid
lag: computer experiencing slow response
lol: laughs out loud
ly: Love ya
np: No problem
omg: oh my god!
relog: To Log out of SL and Log back in.
rez/rezzing: object(s) in process of appearing
rofl: Rolls on Floor Laughing.
sim: a geographic region
tp: Teleport
ty: Thank you
wfm: Works for me
yw: You're welcome

COMMON SECOND LIFE ACRONYMS

L$: Linden Dollar
AR: Abuse Report
CS: Community Standard
FPS[1]: First Person Shooter
FPS[2]: Frames per second
HI: Help Island
HUD: Heads Up Display
IM: Instant Message
LL: Linden Lab
LM: A Landmark to a specific Place.
LSL: Linden Scripting Language
M: Mature Audience
OI: Orientation Island
PG: Parental Guidance (general audience)
RL: Real Life
RPG: Role-Playing Game
SL: Second Life
SLURL: A SL address location
TG: Teen Grid, restricted to 13-17yr olds.
TOS: Terms of Service
TH: Telehub, landing point on Private Islands
UI: User Interface
UUID: Unique ID key for Avatars, Texture, Objects
WA: Welcome Area

COMMON SEARCH WORDS

Sandbox: Public Building Location
Casino: Gambling Available
Mall: Shopping Area
Combat: Supporting Weapons and Combat
Weapons: Products of Destruction
Camping: Paid to sit on land to increase Traffic
Money Tree: Some L$ for New Residents
Free Stuff or Free: Pick up Freebie stuff
Skin: Avatar bodies
Club: Discos, Casinos, Bars, Private Clubs
Beach: Swimwear, boats, pools, Ocean activities
Museum: Traditional, Educational. Art
Library: Traditional, SL related, etc.
Boats: Yachts, live aboard, rentals, slips
Park: Amusement, Animal, Recreational

DEFINITION OF COMMON TERMS

Alpha (Alpha Channels/Alpha Textures): Referring to transparency in images. A 32-bit tga (targa) format file is used when uploading transparencies into Second Life.

Alternate Account (alt): An additional Avatar on the same credit card and used by the same resident. Often used for a secondary activity or accounting. Accusing another resident of being an alt is also impolite.

Appearance: Your Avatar may be changed by right-clicking yourself and choosing "Appearance" which allows you to modify the Avatars sex, physical size, features, and clothes using the modification tools provided.

Attachment: A Prim or object can be joined to (and detached from) your Avatar at about 30 different points. Also see Heads-Up-Display (HUD).

Auto-Return: Landowners can set their land to "auto-return", so that other people's objects will be returned to them after a set time. This prevents their land from getting cluttered with objects.

Avatar: A humanoid representation of your presence in Second Life.

Axis: Refers to a coordinate system. Objects can be moved along different axes while in edit mode. The three basic axes in Second Life are **X (back/forward, horizontal)**, **Y (left/right, horizontal)**, and **Z (up/down, vertical)**.

Basic Account: It's a free account offered by Linden Lab that allows you to have an Avatar and access to all of Second Life except for Land ownership.

Blog: A website that acts like a public email that is often used like a diary. Many Second Life residents (including Lindens) have blogs.

Born: Date account was created and visible on the Avatar's **profile**. Residents celebrate their born date as a second birthday. They also wish each other Happy Rez Day.

Camping: Refers to the practice of a resident remaining in one location and not interacting with the world. This property-sitting is often "paid" for by a landowner wishing to increase their Traffic score.

Charter (Charter Members): Account holders who have been with Second Life since the beginning days and their profiles state it.

Charters (Group Charters): Groups have a Charter that is set by the group officers; it provides a description of the group, the purpose and what the group is about.

Community Standards (CS): The rules of the SL world to ensure peaceful and tolerant interaction among the residents. CS defines what behavior is acceptable and unacceptable in this community.

Coordinates: A position in 3D space represented in the form of a vector (x, y, z). Coordinates of your Avatar in-world are visible at the top of the screen next to the Sim name. These coordinates represent your "local" position in the sim (not "global").

Damage/Not Safe: Settings found in designated combat locations. Means residents can be harmed and/or die on that parcel of land. If your Avatar dies you are teleported home and your health is regenerated.

Edge: Is an invisible boundary wall an Avatar bounces off of when there is no more sim

Estate: A collection of one or more regions. Assembling regions as an Estate provides the landowners with specific tools to facilitate managing multiple regions more easily.

Face: Can be the Avatar's face; but also refers to the side(s) of a Prim.

First Land: A residents with paid membership (called premium account) used to be allowed to make an initial land purchase of a 512m2 plot of land at a drastically reduced rate.

First Person Shooter (FPS): A reference found when gaming involves combat. It refers to shooting when a player is playing against another.

Flexible: An **Edit** property that can be applied to a Prim causing it to "flex" either with movement or by being blown by the wind. This property is used when making hair, clothing, flags, etc. flow realistically.

Flex-Prim: A Prim with settings that allows it to react to gravity, wind, and motion. Typically used for flags, hair, and clothes.

Frames Per Second (FPS): Notation on how fast your computer is updating your display. The higher the FPS the better the clarity and smoothness of your display feed. Lag can reduce FPS and slow your system's reaction time down.

Furry or Anthropomorphism (anthro): The Avatars which use Prim attachments to look like certain animal or mythical creature while keeping their basic humanoid framework.

Gesture: A combination of animation, pose, text and sound that can be triggered by shortcuts. Lower right hand menu tab labeled **Gestures** can be clicked to engage a particular gesture. Look under **Inventory: Gestures:** *right click* **Create New Gestures** for ideas on how to create your own.

Grey: References the grey color you see on your display before the feed to your computer is complete.

Grid: Refers to Second Life's world which is made up of a collection of networked servers that run sims.

Grief (Griefer): Means to cause great distress or to abuse another resident in SL. Rule of thumb: "treat others as you would like to be treated". For example, do not cage, push, destroy, or call names.

Heads-Up Display (HUD): is an attachment point on an Avatar which allows an object to be visible only to the User whose Avatar it is attached to. There are 8 HUD attachment points that can be used for display.

Help Island: A Linden Lab location where you can find instructions on how second life works.

Home: A resident's home location. Can be set from the **World** menu, but works only if the user is over land they own individually or as part of a Group.

Island (referred also to as Private Island or Estate): Refers to the purchase of an entire region. These can be connected to other regions, or they can be independent regions and even surrounded by water or void space.

Key: Keyboard character. Also see **Universal Unique Identifier (UUID)**

Lag: Refers to the delay felt when there is a slow or faulty internet connection. This can happen when there are too many Avatars or physical interaction of things trying to take place at once.

Liaisons: Linden staffers who spend their time predominantly in-world, helping Residents and ensuring that the grids run smoothly. They also monitor the Live Help channel for calls that need an immediate Linden response.

Linden Lab (LL): The company that created Second Life. LL was founded in 1999 by Philip Rosedale (Philip Linden) and originally located at 333 Linden Street, San Francisco (hence the name "Linden").

Linden Dollar (L$): The virtual economic currency in Second Life. L$ can be traded for USD (United States currency) and vice versa via the LindeX service.

Linden Scripting Language (LSL): The built-in scripting language used in Second Life. A C/Java-like language which is used to have an object interact with other objects and with the residents in-world.

Machinima (muh-sheen-eh-mah): Animated movies involving the use of game engines and virtual worlds. A movie made in the Second Life world is referred to as Machinima.

Mainland: The main land mass on the Main Grid. It's usually the largest contiguous area of land.

Mature: Certain behavior is allowed only in "Mature" sims, such as profanity, nudity, and sexual content and must not be seen by the world.

Newbie: An inexperienced or new resident. Also referred to as a "new user"," newcomer" or "noob".

Non-player character (NPC): A character in a role-playing game or computer game whose actions are not controlled by a human player.

Object: Is one or more primitive shapes (Prims).

Off-world: When an object or Avatar is out of the bounds of the grid. When this happens to an Avatar, it will be trapped in what feels like "empty space". Objects are returned to **Inventory** and Avatars have to relog.

Orientation Island (OI): Where new players begin when they enter Second Life.

Packet Loss: Due to bad network lines and/or hardware failure "packets" (referring to the transfer of data via the Internet) get damaged or lost.

Parental Guidance (PG): Does not involve Parents but the common designation is known for no Nudity, sexual content (even paintings), and profanity in the Sim. (Violence such as damage-enabled land and weapons are still allowed where designated)

Permissions: Properties applied to items and dictates what other residents can do to that item.

Prim: Refers to a "primitive" 3D polygonal shapes (Cube, Prism, Sphere, Tube, ring, Torus, etc.) used by residents to build objects in Second Life.

Pie Menu (Options Menu): The round menu that appears with options when you *right click* on objects or Avatars (command-clicking on Macs).

Prim (Primitive): A single cube or sphere or other shape is counted as one Prim. Link them together and the object Prim count then becomes the sum of those shapes. Each land parcel has a Prim Limit.

Primfficiency: Mastering the art (and science) of Prim shaping to minimize Prim count.

Private Island: Residents can purchase an entire region that is usually separate from the mainland and provides far greater control over access and terrain design.

QuickTime: The video streaming technology that interfaces with Second Life and allows the user to view content in-world. You must have Quicktime installed for you to participate in viewing.

Rating: Given by other residents to show appreciation for another resident's creations or skills in certain fields (behavior, appearance, and building). A resident's ratings can be seen in their profile.

Real life (RL): A term used in virtual games that refers to the actual physical real world that we all eat, sleep, and live in.

Region: Land masses 256m by 256m are called Regions or Sims. If you look on the Map, you will clearly see these divided masses throughout the grid, each Region has a unique name and is rated Mature or PG.

Resident: Is an individual who has a membership (thus an Avatar) in Second Life.

Rez or Rezzing: Is a term used when an Object is in the process of "appearing".

Sandbox: This is public access space that is available for anyone to build on. Sandboxes are cleared of objects automatically, twice per day. The signs make it clear what is and is not allowed in a particular sandbox.

Sim (Simulator): Often used synonymous with Region. However, a "Sim" is actually a reference to an SL server that runs simulations of one or more regions. A sim is 256m x 256m (65,536 sq m) area in Second Life.

Skin: Refers to a custom skin or more accurately a texture that is applied to an Avatar to make it look more realistic. These custom skins can have muscle tone, skin coloring, tattoos, and makeup.

SLURL: Refers to the direct teleport link to a location in Second Life. On websites and blogs it is often represented as a Map that will link start Second Life. Second Life membership is required to enable this function.

Stipend: An allowance of Linden Dollars ($L) paid out weekly to eligible Residents.

Texture: An image that covers Prims and can look like material or a picture of an object. Textures are also used to make clothing.

Town Hall: Town Hall meetings are announced and held by Linden Lab to discuss Second Life topics. These meetings encourage Resident participation with questions.

Traffic: A way Second Life tracks the most popular locations. Landowners can earn a "Popular Place" listing in the Search screen for the day if their Traffic count the previous day was in the top 20 of all Traffic Counts. Traffic is an additive amount of time spent by each Avatar.

Transparent: Objects can be made to be seen through, They are usually made of Prims that have a transparency setting or have a transparent texture.

Teleport (TP): Is when you go from one location to another instantaneously.

Tier Fee: A monthly land payment, similar to a property tax, that is due to Linden Lab on land you own. The first 512 sq meters of land held does not require a Tier fee payment.

User Interface (UI): Is the software application on your computer that talks to the SL server.

Universal Unique Identifier (UUID): Items and Avatars' unique reference number. (In string form it looks like this "00000000-0000-0000-0000-000000000000" or something like this "76554f3c-g055-d9c8-066d-e6475r6rdtb2"). If someone else knows your key it does **NOT** mean they can harm or have access to your personal account information.

Void regions/Sim: Refers to the landless areas supported by the server. For example, the water or air regions owned by Governor Linden, that are held to provide public flight and sailing areas.

SCREEN COMMANDS

File Edit View World Tools Help ⚔ Help Island 3 186, 173, 22 (PG) - Sandbox - Play Here! 12:45 PM PST ⚫ LSO

MENU BAR
(*Left-click* for a drop menu or use the **Alternative Command Shortcuts** noted)

FILE:

Upload Image (L$10): Import textures into Second Life, from your hard drive. **(Ctrl-U)**

Upload Sound (L$10): Import small audio clips into Second Life (10 second max)

Upload Animation (L$10): Import animations and poses from Poser software.

Bulk Upload (L$10): Easy way to upload of group of images. Does not allow for preview.

Close Window: Will close the window currently open. **(Ctrl-W)**

Save Texture As: Lets you save textures and snapshots from your inventory back onto your hard drive.

Take Snapshot: Take a snapshot of what you are currently looking at and save it. **(Ctrl-Shift-S)**

Snapshot to Disk: Take and save a snapshot to hard drive, not your inventory. **(Ctrl-')**

Start/Stop Movie to Disk: Record what you are seeing as a video file to your hard drive. **(Ctrl-Shift-A)**

Set Window Size: Adjust the SL window size for making movies.

Quit: Logs out of Second Life. **(Ctrl-Q)**

EDIT:

Undo: This will undo the last build action you if the object is still selected. **(Ctrl-Z)**

Redo: Redo the previously Undo build action. **(Ctrl-Y)**

Cut: Cuts text, for pasting like in a Note. **(Ctrl-X)**

Copy: Copy text for Notes or copy Items in your Inventory for pasting. **(Ctrl-C)**

Paste: Paste the copied (or the cut) text and items. **(Ctrl-V)**

Delete: Delete the selected text or inventory object. **(Del)**

Search: Opens the Search window. **(Ctrl-F)**

Select All: Selects all text in the area you are using. **(Ctrl-A)**

Deselect: This deselects previously selected text. **(Ctrl-E)**

Duplicate: Creates a copy of object when its in Edit mode. **(Ctrl-D)**

Attach Object: Attach objects (hair, accessories, weapons, etc) to your body.

Detach Object: Removes the attachments from your body.

Take Off Clothing: Removes one piece of clothing, or all clothes.

Gestures: Opens the Gestures window. **(Ctrl-G)**

Profile: Opens your Profile window.

Appearance: Opens the Appearance window for customizing your Avatar.

Friends: Displays your Friends List. **(Ctrl-Shift-F)**

Groups: Shows your Group list.

Preferences: Opens Preferences window for adjusting your SL settings. **(Ctrl-P)**

VIEW:

Mouselook: See the view through the eyes of your Avatar. **(M)***

Build: This will open build mode. **(B)***

Reset View: Resets *mouselook* and camera views back to a normal view. **(Escape Key)**

Look At Last Chatter: Turns your Avatar's head to look at the Avatar who last spoke in chat. **(Ctrl-\)**

Toolbar: Toggles the buttons at the bottom of the screen on and off.

Chat History: Show or hide the Chat History since sign on. **(Ctrl-H)**

Instant Message: Show or hide the Instant Message window. **(Ctrl-T)**

Inventory: Show or hide the Inventory window. **(Ctrl-I)**

Mute List: View the list of residents and objects that you muted.

Camera Controls: Small pop up window giving mouse access to the camera controls.

Movement Controls: Shows or hides a small window giving mouse access to the movement controls.

World Map: Opens and closes the world map. **(Ctrl-M)**

Mini-Map: Opens and closes the mini-map that shows the immediate area. **(Ctrl-Shift-M)**

Statistics Bar: Opens and closes the Statistics Bar. **(Ctrl-Shift-1)**

Property Lines: Shows land boundaries as red lines on the landscape. **(Ctrl-Alt-Shift-P)**

Land Owners: Indicates ownership: you (green), your group (teal), for sale (orange) other people (red).

Hover Tips: Shows information about objects your mouse touches. **(Ctrl-Shift-T)**

Alt Shows Physical: When checked, holding the Alt key down will display physical objects in red **(Alt)**

Highlight Transparent: Makes the transparent objects visible in a translucent red. **(Ctrl-Alt-T)**

Beacons: Shows a beacon on the coordinates of objects with script, sound, physical, and emitting particles.

Show HUD Attachments: If unchecked, HUDs are not up on your screen; but they respond to commands.

Zoom In: Moves the camera view closer in. **(Ctrl-0)**

Zoom Default: Sets the camera zoom to the default. **(Ctrl-9)**

Zoom Out: Moves the camera view farther out. **(Ctrl-8)**

Toggle Fullscreen: Toggles between running Second Life in a window, or as a full screen. **(Alt-Enter)**

Set UI Size to Default: Returns the UI, which is scalable, to 1.00.

*Make sure **Chat** is closed when using a single letter command.

WORLD:

Chat: Toggles the chat bar used for talking to residents close by.

Start Gesture: Symbol starts a gesture command order in the chat bar. **(/)**

Always Run: Toggles run mode on and off, so that you can choose whether to walk or to run **(Ctrl-R)**

Fly: Toggles the fly and stop flying command. **(Home key)**

Create Landmark Here: Create a landmark marking your current location.

Set Home to Here: Set as your position as Home (if land settings give you permission).

Teleport Home: Teleports you immediately back to your set Home location. **(Ctrl-Shift-H)**

Set Away: Setting communicates to those around that you are "away from keyboard." Movement releases it. **(afk)**

Set Busy: Setting tells others not to interrupt. If you receive an IM a Busy message is relayed.

Account History: Displays your Account History window.

Manage My Account: Directs you to the SL website for more options in managing your account.

Buy L$: Accesses LindeX, the currency exchange system for buying and selling Linden Dollars.

My Land: Opens the My Land window summarizing your land information. Allows you to teleport there.

About Land: Opens About Land window on the land you are currently over.

Buy Land: If the land you are currently on is For Sale, it brings up the Buy land window for purchasing it.

Region/Estate: Window for managing land textures, access, weather and day/night cycles.

Force Sun: Change the time of day which affects the lighting for your view.

Noon: The best setting to see everything in-world **(Ctrl-Shift-Y)**

Sunset: Sometimes best for Snapshots and non-harsh lighting **(Ctrl-Shift-N)**

TOOLS:

Some commands only work when an object is selected with **Build: Edit (Ctrl-3)**

Select Tool: Directly opens Build to the selected tool. Toggle Build Open/Close **(B)**; Close window **(esc)**

Focus: Brings object focus to the center of the screen **(Ctrl-1)**, Orbit **(Ctrl)**, Pan **(Ctrl-Shift)**

Move: Allows you to move your objects freely **(Ctrl-2)**; Lift **(Ctrl)**; Spin **(Ctrl-Shift)**

Edit: Used to position and Size Objects **(Ctrl-3)**; Rotate **(Ctrl)**; Stretch **(Ctrl-Shift)**

Create: Opens the Build window **(Ctrl-4)** Toggle Open/Close the Build window **(B)**

Land: Owner controlled command window to edit terrain, join parcels, etc. **(Ctrl-5)**

Select Only My Objects: When checked, will only recognize the objects you own.

Select Only Movable Objects: Allows selection of only your moveable objects.

Show by Surrounding: The highlighted selection box will show objects that are in it's boundaries.

Show Hidden Selection: In Edit all vertices even those hidden behind or in objects are highlighted.

Show Light Radius for Selection: The radius of the light will be shown by a transparent sphere.

Show Selection Beam: When selecting the selection beam can be seen.

Snap To Grid: Toggles the grid rulers used when dragging objects; then allows the option to snap **(G)**

Snap Object XY To Grid: Select object(s) and then snap it to the X and Y axis, not Z **(Shift-X)**

Use Selection For Grid: Used by experienced builders, resets the grid reference to an object. **(Shift-G)**

Grid Options: Grid Options window for changing grid spacing for the World grid. **(Ctrl-Shift-B)**

Link: Create a single object by selecting the objects (Shift-*click*) in Edit mode and choose Link **(Ctrl-L)**

Unlink: Simply Edit (Ctrl-3) the object and choose Unlink **(Ctrl-shift L)**

Stop All Animation: Useful for turning animation of your Avatar off **(/ao)**

Focus On Selection: Immediately snaps camera center on the selected object (in Edit mode) **(H)**

Zoom To Selection: Zooms in on selected object (in Edit mode) **(Shift-H)**

Take: If you have permission, this will take the object into your inventory.

Take Copy: Takes a copy of the object into your inventory, and leaves the selected one in-world.

Save Object Back To My Inventory: Saves the changes on object back to inventory while working on it.

Save Object Back To Object Contents: Take an object from contents and edit it and save changes back.

Show Script Warning/Error Window: Pops open Script window for auditing error/warning.

Recompile Scripts In Selection: Forces a recompile of any scripts within the selected object (Edit mode)

Reset Scripts In Selection: Resets the state of any scripts in a selected object.

Set Scripts to Running in Selection: Turns the script on if it is not already running.

Set Scripts to Not Running in Selection: Turns running scripts off within the selected object.

HELP:
Second Life Help: Access the Help information **(F1)**

Knowledge Base: Asks permission to open your browser to the Second Life web site for information.

Contact Support: Asks to direct you to the Second Life web site for an email form.

Official Linden Blog: Shortcut to the Official Linden Blog page.

Scripting Guide: Provides some in-world scripting information.

Scripting Wiki: Brings up the official support site with more in depth scripting documentation.

Message of the Day: The same message received at login, this link gives it to you again.

Reporting Abuse: Format used to report violations of the Terms of Service and Community Standards.

Bumps, Pushes, and Hits: Not sure? This window tells you if you had a Bump, Push, or Hit.

Report Bug: Use to report technical features that are not performing right.

Help Request: Allows you to get help through IM from a Live Help member.

Release Notes: Links you to a list of the updates in the last release.

About Second Life: Window stating Software version, credits and other information.

BUTTON BAR

Left-click the blue buttons on the bottom of your screen or use the **Alternative Command Shortcuts** noted

HISTORY (Opens with Chat): Reads what has been said in Chat **(Ctrl-H)**

IM: Hold a private conversation with a specified person **(Ctrl-T)**

CHAT: Talk publicly to people nearby

> **Say:** Relays Chat within normal voice distance **(Enter)**

> **Shout:** Relays Chat farther away even the next Sim **(Ctrl-Enter)**

FRIENDS: Find and communicate with your buddies **(Ctrl-Shift-F)**

FLY: Get around faster by air. Use E/C or Pg Up/Pg Down **(Shift-F)**

SNAPSHOT: Save a screen shot to your computer or inventory **(Ctrl-Shift-S)**

SEARCH: Find places, events, people, and more **(Ctrl-F)**

> **All:** Select ALL Search categories listed below

> **Classifieds:** Paid Advertising. Higher amount paid gets higher listing.

> **Events:** Free Advertising for special events.
> Event time is 3 hours max.

> **Popular Places:** Top 20 high traffic locations. List updated daily.

> **Land Sales:** Lists land that is for sale and available at auction.

> **Places:** Land name, classification, and listing as set by Land Owner.

BUTTON BAR (Cont.)

BUILD: Create New Objects **(B)**

     Focus: (Ctrl-1)

     Move: (Ctrl-2)

     Edit: (Ctrl-3)

     Create: (Ctrl-4)

     Land: (Ctrl-5)

MINI-MAP: Map of the area around you **(Ctrl-Shift-M)**

MAP: Map of the World **(Ctrl-M)**

INVENTORY: File containing your items **(Ctrl-I)**

GESTURES: List of Active Avatar Gestures. Click on a Gesture to "Play".